Rebellion of Silence

BY ROBERT MASSINGILL JR.

**A DRAMATIC TRUE STORY OF A CHILD
WHO HAD A SEED OF REBELLION
AND PLOTTED TO DESTROY
THE SCHOOL HE ATTENDED.
AS GOD AND SATAN ENGAGED IN WARFARE
OVER HIS SOUL, THE WAR RAGED WITHIN
HIM. WHO WOULD FINALLY PREVAIL IN HIS
LIFE, GOD OR SATAN? WILL THE STORY END
IN SPIRITUAL DEATH, OR SPIRITUAL LIFE?**

Bookman Publishing
Martinsville, Indiana

ISBN: 1-932301-99-2

PREFACE

HE STARTED OUT IN SCHOOL LIKE ANY OTHER INNOCENT CHILD. THEN, THROUGH A SERIES OF TRAUMATIC EVENTS, HE HAD A BAD RELATIONSHIP WITH A TEACHER. HE DEVELOPED A DEADLY HATRED FOR THE SCHOOL, THAT WITHOUT GOD'S SUPERNATURAL INTERVENTION, HE WOULD HAVE GONE TO THE POINT OF NO RETURN.

PROLOGUE

Have you ever wondered what goes through the mind of a criminal? Have you ever wondered what causes a child to have a criminal mind? Have you ever wondered what goes through the mind of a child when he or she is disciplined? Have you ever wondered what goes through the mind of a nine year old kid when he is scolded unfairly, either by a parent, or a school teacher?

I suppose we all ask these questions at one time or another. However, it is not my intention by writing this book, to make excuses for bad behavior. We all have to take responsibility for our actions.

You remember in the Garden of Eden when Adam ate the forbidden fruit? Adam tried to lay it off on Eve. He said to God, "The woman You gave me, she gave it to me and I did eat."

Eve laid it off on the serpent. She said to God, "The serpent beguiled me and I did eat" (Gen. 3:12-13). So, it is the nature of man to not to want to take responsibility for his actions.

However, on the other hand, Eve also was banished from the garden. If Adam was the one who was fully responsible for what happened, why couldn't Eve continue to live in the garden? Because she sinned also. Then, where do we lay the blame? God divided the blame between all of them, including the serpent.

The following is a true story about a certain child, who had an encounter with a certain school teacher on seemingly negative terms. This is not to say that the teacher was intentionally mean to the child. But it is to say that an unhappy relationship between a school teacher and a child can sow seeds in the child's life that can have devastating results.

Throughout the text I will be sharing certain events that may sound negative on the surface, but it is not meant to be negative. I'm just simply sharing the events that occurred as I remember them; not that I am remembering it against them in some way. It is by no means the intent of this book to send a negative message about school teachers. School teachers are good people. They are very important to society. But like the rest of us, they are human. They're not perfect. They cannot always read the mind of their students. They cannot always discern the emotions of a child with whom they have dealings with.

I certainly do not have all the answers to these things. In fact, I'm not even sure I have any answers. I may not even know what I'm talking about. I am not a physiologist. I have trouble spelling the word, much less know anything about the professional field. I have never raised any children. So, what advice could I give about raising children?

I suppose I don't have much to offer except to say that I was a child once. I have had some experience at being a child. In retrospect, it was a crash course, I suppose, but at least I've been there.

It is my opinion that there are basically three groups of people that to some extent, collectively (to what extent, I'm not sure) control human destiny. These three groups are as follows: spiritual leaders such as preachers, Sunday school teachers, and youth workers in the church. The other two are parents and school teachers. For the most part, I will be focusing on school teachers in this story.

I will use an illustration to make my point: hypothetically speaking, let's say that you were sitting before a desk in a high tower. Before you is a wide control board covered with buttons. God tells you that he has given you the power to run the world from this control board. If you push a certain button, it will rain. If you push a certain button, it will be cloudy, or if you push a certain button, it will snow and so forth and so on. But there are certain buttons that you can push and do devastating damage to the Earth. For instance, there is a certain button that if pushed, would wipe out a major city with a volcano. You could destroy the entire planet if you pushed a certain button. Then God says to you, "Don't push any of these certain buttons." God gives you the wisdom and intelligence to push all the right buttons at the right time. But you are human. You're still not perfect. Although you have the knowledge to always hit the right button, you could make a mistake. Then God tells you, "Always get a good nights sleep before coming to work. Don't come in here half asleep. Don't have a fight with your husband or wife, which ever it is, and then, come in here in a bad mood. These things may cause you to hit the wrong button and do devastating damage to the Earth."

You've probably never thought about it this way, but in a sense, the three groups of people I mentioned above are in this position. Everyday, school teachers make choices and decisions about how they are going to handle a given situation in a child's life. They may make the best decision they know how to make for the moment. They could make a mistake and push the wrong button and cause the child to be a little discouraged. But in many cases, the child will get over it. Probably no damage is done.

But what if the teacher had a bad day and hit a destructive button in a child's life in a vulnerable moment, provoked the child to anger, and the child grew up to be a serial killer? Or maybe not that bad, maybe he became a thief, or some other kind of criminal. Maybe he didn't become a criminal at all. Maybe when he grew up, he treated his children cruel, and they grew up to be criminals. Then, again maybe he completely recovered from it and no damage was done at all.

The story that I have to offer should send a message to everyone who works with children, to learn to be more sensitive with the emotional needs of a child. The story is about a boy who started out in school just like any other kid. Outwardly, he appeared to be as innocent as any of the other kids. But inwardly, he was filled with a spirit of rebellion against the school that grew in him like a demon.

How do I know this is a true story? Because the child I am writing about is myself. All of the names of the players in this story are fictional except for the author, and his immediate family members and relatives. Also the names in this book which are preceded by the mark, `*` are real. The names of schools and geographical locations are also real.

Many times when we are in church, we hear testimonies from people about how God saved them. We hear all kinds of stories about how God delivered someone from excessive alcohol addiction or from drugs, tobacco, and a host of other problems. We've heard it said many times that God works in mysterious ways. How true it is! We've also heard it said that God deals with different people in many different ways. He deals with one person one way and another person another way. So now, if you continue reading, you are about to read about another wild story to add to that list.

CONTENTS

CHAPTER ONE
STAGE OF INNOCENCE

Atcooga school was located about a quarter of a mile south of Dalton Georgia on highway forty-one. I suppose you could consider it a small school. In those days it never crossed my mind that it was a small school. It only had grades from the first through the eighth. It had one room for each grade except that it did not have a room for the third grade. Some of the third grade students were in the second grade room, and some were in the fourth grade room. Also, the seventh and eighth grades were in the same room. I remember on the south end of the hall, there was the handy-capped class for the kids who were slow learners or handy-capped in some way.

I will always remember the school yard with it's large and gentle oak and hardwood trees spaced out over the area. I remember the ground being covered with the brown and golden leaves that fell in the fall. Some of the boys used to pile them up and jump out of the swings into the big piles.

It was a sunshinny day in the fall of 1958 when I enrolled in the first grade at the yellow school building. Mama and I walked a mile or so to the school for that purpose. I remember my shoe sole falling halfway off before we got there.

Up until now, I had always wanted to go to school, but I was too young. It may be that I wanted to go because my two older sisters, Patricia (we called her Pat) and Dorothy went. I remember once Daddy (he was a big built man with black hair, weighing about 200 pounds) telling me, "It'll be years before you can go to school." Now, finally, the time had come.

I was doing very well in school in the first grade. I learned my A B C's quickly. My teacher, Mrs. Dyer, a young slim lady with lengthy brown hair taught us to make figures to one hundred. I got far ahead. I would go to 150 or further. I was doing so well that she thought to have me double promoted to the second grade.

For some reason the principal, Mr. Busby, a medium built, elderly man with short gray hair would not go along with it. He was afraid it might not work out.

Every morning, the teacher would sharpen pencils for the students. The pencil sharpener was too high up on the wall for us to reach. I remember a certain dark headed boy, who would take his ink pen to her and want it sharpened. I can remember her exclaiming to him, "Anthony, I can't sharpen a pen!"

I had a lot of friends in this school. There was a certain boy about my size, named Clyde Ashton, who was in my room. We played together a lot. We competed with each other, as to whoever was the bravest, or whoever was the strongest, or whatever the game happened to be. We wrestled and played like kids normally do. He stands out tall in my memories of those days.

All children need discipline sometimes. In my first grade class, it was everyday's business. There was almost always at least one or more that was getting into some kind of mischief. In the cloak room, there was blocks that we played with during recess, when we couldn't go outside. Many times, some of the boys had a bad habit of staying in the cloak room playing with blocks after recess was over. They would get away with it until the blocks fell over. I can remember occasions when we would be in class, and then, we would hear the rumbling of the blocks hitting the floor. Then, the guilty boys would come walking out of the cloak room, one by one. On one occasion, I hid back there by myself, and was playing with the blocks. I had tried to get a certain girl named Wendy who sat in front of me to hide back there with me, but she wouldn't. I remember her having long blonde hair. She said to me, speaking of the teacher, "She might haul off."

When Mrs. Dyer caught me, she got the yard stick after me, and sent me to my seat. I remember feeling embarrassed.

One warm sunny day when recess was over, all the kids went in but me. I stayed outside at the slide by myself. I climbed the ladder and slid down the slide, over and over, all by myself. Then, I looked around and there stood Mrs. Dyer. She didn't say anything verbally, but she sternly pointed to the front entrance of the school. I knew what she meant, so I started toward the front door. When I walked in, she again pointed sternly down the hall in the direction of our class room. When we walked down the hall to the room, she again pointed toward the door of the class room, and I went inside.

Now Anthony, the boy who wanted his pen sharpened, was one who would get sent to the principal's office a lot of times. He would get a paddling, but it seemed that he hardly ever showed emotion.

There was some kind of sandwich meat we ate at home a lot of times. It was called side meat. I don't remember if it was cooked or not, but the thought came to my mind about Anthony not ever crying when he got a paddling. I thought to myself, "He must eat `bottom meat."

But what I didn't realize about most of Mr. Busby's paddlings, was that he only pretended to paddle. He just gave little love taps that really amounted to nothing.

At this point in my life, if I was disciplined by a teacher, I had no rebellion against it that I recall being aware of. I got into trouble a few times. I had a habit of putting dirt on the slide. When other kids came down the slide, they would slide through a pile of dirt. I was told over and over not to do that, but I did it anyway. One day I did it, and Mrs. Dyer said to me, "Come with me."

We were walking toward the front of the school building. I was curious and kept asking her, "Where're we going?"

She said sternly, "You're coming with me."

We went into our classroom, and I was sitting in a desk. The principal's office was across the hall. As she was standing in the doorway of our room, I realized that she was taking me to the principal's office. Then, I started crying, and tried to talk her out of it.

We went into the office, and then, Mr. Busby told me to wash my hands in the sink. He wasn't mad at all, he talked nice to me. But he said to me, "We're gonna give you a little paddling." It didn't seem little to me at the time, and it didn't do any good when I tried to talk him out of it. I quit putting dirt on the slide.

The school year came and went. The next year I started in the second grade. I got along very well with my second grade teacher, Mrs. Parker, who seemed to me to be middle aged (she was older than Mrs. Dyer) with medium length brown hair. I liked both, her and Mrs. Dyer. Mrs. Dyer was still teaching the first grade, and on occasions I met her on the school ground and talked to her. On one occasion on a sunny day, I was playing like I was running up a big oak tree that stood close to the slide. She was standing close by. I had on a new pair of shoes. She said to me gently, "Don't tear up your new shoes, Robert."

The relationship I had with Mrs. Parker went very well during my second year. But this is not to say that she didn't have rules and discipline. We had our ups and downs. There were times that she scolded the other kids and myself also when we got out of order.

There was a certain boy in my room, named Henry Danton, who was a little taller than I was, and had brown hair that was combed to one side. He and I became friends and we played together a lot. Clyde Ashton was also in our room, and we were still friends. There were three other boys that we all were friends with; Kelly Lacky, Tony Shields, and Wallace Daniels. We all used to play tag a lot and chase each other. Kelly was taller than I was and had blonde hair. Tony was about my size and had brown hair. Wallace was a little lighter weight than I was, and had brownish blonde hair.

One day, right after we had been doing a lot of running, we had just come into the classroom. We had just taken our seats when I heard one of the kids saying as he laughed, "Look at Wallace's face." I looked around at him and saw black lines all in his face where he had smeared the dirt and sweat.

One rainy day, I don't remember what we were supposed to be doing, but Kelly, Tony, and I were running across the back area of the playground. There may have been some of the others with us. Tony and Kelly were running side by side. Then they tripped on each other, and fell down on the muddy ground. Not meaning any harm or offense to either of them, I laughed because of what what happened. Kelly, having a nice personality, didn't seem to mind because I laughed at them. But Tony, being a little more rigid, scowled and said, "He's laughing!," as they went to the bathroom to wash off.

I remember once on a sunny day, when we had just come in from recess, the teacher was scolding a certain boy for running out in front of a car. Behind the school playground there was a side street. It wasn't a street that anyone would be likely to drive fast on. She said to him to the effect, "That man had to stop so fast it killed his engine. Now, why'd you do that, Jamie?"

The boy who was heavy set, with short dark hair replied, "I didn't see it."

This excuse wasn't acceptable to Mrs. Parker. There had been many times that she had admonished the class not to run out in the street without looking. She sternly asked him again, "Now why'd you do that, Jamie?"

He replied with the same excuse, "I didn't see it."

She continued to scold him until she felt that she had made her point with him.

There were times that I had a strong imagination. For instance, one day she gave us an assignment to go home after school and list as many words as we could that started with an S. There were many times that she gave us these types of assignments. The average amount of words a student would have would probably be anywhere from forty to eighty.

On this particular occasion, I really got in to it. I went home and looked everywhere, in the newspapers and wherever I could and numbered 312 words. After I had collected them, I got to thinking. In my mind, I imagined her getting mad because I listed so many. It seemed like she might think I cheated. In my mind's eye, I could see her standing beside my desk with an angry frown, saying, "What'd you do?"

When I went to school the next day, I hid them and did not turn them in. Wallace, who sat across the aisle from me asked me, "How many words did you get?"

I replied, "Eighty-eight."

In the process of things, she never did come around to see how many we had, and she didn't take them up. I never did tell her or anyone how many I had. But every time I hear the figure 312, I always remember this scene.

I had trouble learning to play baseball. I couldn't hit the ball. There was another game I liked, called roll-e-bat. Someone would hit the ball and then they would lay the bat on the ground. Whoever got it would roll the ball on the ground from where they picked it up, and try to hit the bat. If they hit the bat, they would be up to bat. But the trouble was, they wouldn't play my game.

Sometimes the other kids would gripe because I wouldn't strike when they pitched. But if I did hit the ball, I could run the bases well because I was a fast runner. There was a tall, slim, dark headed boy named Alton in our room who was good at hitting the ball. I can remember the popping sound of him hitting the ball and knocking it up in one of the big oak trees that shaded the play ground. So they came up with an idea. When it came my time to bat, they let Alton hit the ball and I ran the bases.

On one occasion, Alton hit the ball and I ran for the first base, then to second. Somewhere between third and forth base, I was caught between two catchers. I ran back and forth between them, as they threw the ball back and forth in an effort to strike me out. At the same time, everyone was shouting in excitement. Then one of them dropped the ball and I made a home run out of it. But in the process of time, I gradually lost interest in sports.

I remember right at the end of the year, Mrs. Parker was scolding a boy named Curt Green for acting up in the classroom. She came back to his desk to correct him. But the boy who was about my size with short, dark hair got mad at her and talked back to her roughly, saying, "Leave me alone! I'll call the police on you, you just wait!"

The rest of us giggled as she said to him, "Oh, you're not gonna call the police."

It seemed funny to me and I pictured her in my mind, standing in the front door of her house, and the police coming down the road to get her.

Then came the third year. When I entered the third grade, I started out in the same classroom I was in before. Mrs. Parker was no longer there and the new teacher's name was Mrs. Mitchell. She walked with a limp and I thought she had a broken leg.

I liked her as I did Mrs. Dyer and Mrs. Parker.

Whenever she disciplined one of the kids, she would call them into the cloak room. For instance, she would say, "Monte, I wanna see you in the cloak room." Then she would take them in there and paddle them. It seemed like to me at the time, she was calling them at random, and it was almost everyday's business.

I was always afraid that I would be next. Every time she would call someone into the cloak room, it would scare me. But she never did call me.

It didn't take long for me to discover that she liked me. One day she smiled at me saying, "You're a hard worker."

On one occasion, I discovered that I had made a mistake on one of my papers. Because I messed up, I thought I was going to get in trouble. I raised my hand, and becoming emotional, said to her to the effect, "Mrs. Mitchell, I'm gonna have to erase part of this because I did it wrong."

"Oh, that's all right," she responded in a kind voice. She went on to explain that it was all right to make mistakes and have to erase them.

The relationship I had with her was short lived. There was some shifting done with the placement of the students and I was sent to the fourth grade room.

The fourth grade teacher's name was Mrs. Thomas. She was a fairly young teacher, probably in her thirties with a nice looking hair-do that was in the brown or blonde class. I already knew her before, because she had been teaching there the previous years. I liked her as I did my other teachers. And also, she had in times past, come to our house and visited us.

There were times that she would scold us if we failed to do all of our work properly, or not pay attention like we should. For instance, one day she had Tony Shields in front of the class correcting him. I was seated on the front row. She said something to him to the effect, "You're gonna have to start studying and paying attention." Then, she bent him over the top of my desk right in front of me and paddled him. Then, she lightly tapped me on the side of my shoulder with the paddle and replied sternly, "And you too!" But I did not get mad at her. I never had any rebellious feelings toward her.

When we rode the school bus, there was a tall boy with dark hair, named Ronald Black who opened and shut the door to let the kids on and off. He also took names of the kids who got out of order.

One day on the bus, there was something funny that happened and everybody was laughing loudly about it. I could not see what they were laughing at from where I was. The story was, as I was told, there was a drunk man walking down the road. As the bus passed by him, he stumbled and fell into the ditch.

I got out of my seat and walked toward the back of the bus to see what was so funny. But still, could not see what happened.

The next morning, I was playing on the swings under the shade of the oak trees in the back section of the playground. Ronald came around to where I was and called me. He said something like, "Robert, com'on. You have to go to the office because I took your name yesterday."

I went into the principal's office with him, and there were several others whose names were taken. They all were sitting around the shellacked table and acted as if they were looking forward to getting a paddling from Mr. Busby. They all were having a good time because they knew that he never paddled hard.

He finally came into the room and lectured all of us about behaving ourselves on the school bus.

A certain girl named Debra got in line and said to the effect, "I'm gonna be first."

It was like we were playing a game. He gave us all a few love taps with his paddle and then we all proceeded to go to our rooms. Then he replied, "Let's not have any laughing and talking on the way to your rooms." But we laughed and talked anyway.

Although there was nothing to this, I felt like it was unfair for Ronald to take my name, and I had a few bad thoughts about it. But it was nothing major; it did not create any rebellion in me that I am aware of.

CHAPTER TWO
TWIST OF TRAUMA

In the mid part of my third year of school, my family moved to a different locality, so we had to switch schools. The name of the school we started going to was Valley Point. It was on highway forty-one several miles south of Atcooga.

I was nervous about changing schools. During Christmas vacation, we got moved into our new house. The first day I went to Valley Point, I remember being filled with fear as the bus pulled up in the paved parking lot in front of the red brick school. In my mind, I did not see a school, I saw a huge monster waiting to devour me when I got off the bus.

The school was much bigger than Atcooga. There were five rooms for each grade. It had a front hall and a back hall, connected by the huge auditorium. Grades three, four, and half of the fifth were on the front hall. The other half of the fifth, the sixth, and the seventh grades were on the back hall. On the south end of the back hall, there were two floors. There were two classrooms downstairs. The downstairs was lower than the ground floor, built about two or three feet in the ground.

My youngest sister, Dorothy, myself and a couple of girls about her age that we knew at Atcooga had to go in the principal's office to be assigned to our classes. I remember them having lengthy blonde hair. While we were waiting on the principal to come into the office, I was sitting in a chair that had wheels on it. When the principal, Mr. Evans, a tall man with dark hair and dark rimmed glasses who seemed to be in his early fifties came in, he said to me to the effect, "I need my chair." When he had done all the necessary paperwork, he asked me, "What's your parents's occupation?"

Then, I asked, "What's that mean?"

He replied, "What kind of work do they do?" Then I explained to him that Daddy was a carpenter.

Mrs. Evans was there, and I wanted to be in her room because she seemed so nice. She was not as tall as her husband, and she had dark brown hair. But she wasn't a teacher, she was an office worker. If she had been a teacher, and I had been assigned to her class, the emotional trauma I was experiencing, certainly would have been erased.

They handed me a sheet of paper, and I noticed 'Mrs. Elkinson' written on the top of the page. I realized that it was the name of my new school teacher. When I first met her, a middle aged lady with dark hair and thick classes, I was terrified of her. She seemed to have a stormy nature. When she talked, she sounded scary to me. As she was talking to Mrs. Evans in the hall, just outside the office, her tone of voice sounded to me like a wolf or some sort of a monster.

I can remember occasions when she would discipline some of the boys, she would take them by the shoulders and shake them in a way that seemed vicious to me. For instance, one morning before class, she grabbed a certain blonde haired boy in the hall for something. He was from one of the other third grade classes. She led him through the door of our classroom viciously shaking him by the shoulders, saying, "You keep your hands to yourself!" I've seen her use her yard stick on some of the boys in what seemed to me at the time, a vicious manner.

She showed me to the classroom and talked nice to me as we got acquainted. Although she talked nice to me, I was petrified with fear inside. As I was sitting in my desk as class begun, tormented with a spirit of fear, I remember her saying in a plesant tone to the class, "Well we'd better get started with our work."

The atmosphere in this school was dramatically different to me than it was at Atcooga. I don't know how to explain it, but

DIAGRAM 1
CAMPUS LAYOUT

```
I---------I                    I---------------------------------------------I
I SECOND- I                    I                    MAIN                     I
I   ARY   I                    I                 BUILDING                    I
I         I---------------I    I                                             I
I  BLDG   I               I    I                                             I
I         I---------------I    I              HIGH SCHOOL                    I
I         I               I    I                                             I
I         I               I    I                                             I
I---------I                    I---------------------------------------------I


      I-------------------------------------------------------------I
      I                              DRIVEWAY                        I
      I    I---------------------------------------------------I    I    I
   I     I                            OLD                       I    I    I
   I     I    -------------------------------                   I    I
   I     I    I SLAUGHTER HSE.  I LUNCH  I                      I    I
   I     I    -------------------------------                   I    I
   I     I                            ROOM                       I    I
   I     I  NEW   I---------------------------------------I      I    I
   I     I ------- I                 E                    I      I    I
   I     I LUNCH   I                 L                    I      I    I
   I     I ------- I                 E                    I      I    I
   I     I ROOM    I                 M                    I      I    I
   I     I         I---------I       E      I-------------I      I    I
   I    I          I         I       N      I                    I    I
   I    I          I         I       T      I                    I    I
   I    I          I         I       A      I                    I    I
   I    I          I         I       R      I                    I    I
   I    I          I         I       Y      I                    I    I
   I    I          I         I              I                    I    I
   I    I          I---------I       B      I-------------I      I    I
   I    I          I                 L                    I      I    I
   I    I          I                 D                    I      I    I
   I    I          I                 G                    I      I    I
   I    I    I     I                                      I      I    I
   I    I  I I     I---------------------------------------I      I    I
   I     I I                                              I    I    I
    I     II              DRIVEWAY AND                        I    I    I
    I                     PARKING AREA                    I    I    I
     I                                                    I    I    I
     I                                                         I
     I     I---------------------------------I            I
     I   I                                   I          I
     I   I                                 I          I
     I    I                              I          I
     I    I                            I        I
------------------------------------------------------------
                        Highway 41
------------------------------------------------------------
```

13

it seemed like the other kids were somewhat against me in a way. It wasn't like it was before. Everything in my life had become a nightmare. For instance, one day, a boy about my size with dark hair, (I was about four feet and four inches tall with black hair) named Bernard and I were walking down the hall. I don't remember where we were going, or what the occasion was, but as far as I remember, I was walking a little fast. He said to me in what seemed to me like a sarcastic tone, "We don't do that in this school."

In the process of things, I was under the impression that they had a low profile about people from Atcooga. One day in the lunch line, Mrs. Evans asked me as she was sitting on a stool, punching our lunch tickets, "Do you like our school?" (Now, the lunch room was in a separate building on the west side of the main building.)

I replied, "Yeah."

One of the boys next to me said in a tone that seemed sarcastically to me at the time, "You're supposed to say, `Yes Maam."

At Atcooga, the other kids and I were a family of sorts. Here, it was all different. I remember a certain boy with blonde hair, named Jacob that was a fourth grader in Mrs. Thomas's room. He, myself, and many of the others used to play a game we called `chase.' At the time, I wasn't pronouncing the word right. I was calling it `shase.' Once, when we were grouped at the north end of the building, I said, "Let's play shace."

Jacob said to me, "Say chase."

I knew what he meant. Then I pronounced it correctly. I replied, "Chase," as he returned a smile at me.

I remember once during recess, I walked up behind a certain brown headed boy named Ben. I was trying to play with him, and went about it the wrong way. He did not know I was behind him. Then, I shoved him forward. There was a muddy section of ground in front of him, and he got mud on his shoes. He got mad at me and yelled something to the effect, "If you do that again, you're gonna be in trouble!"

Covering up my embarrassed emotions, I laughed out loud, "Ah, ha ha."

There was a certain boy about my size, named Brian that I got acquainted with. He had brown hair that was a little longer than some of the others. He was a good kid, but I misunderstood him. He always wanted to play wrestle in a way that I wasn't used to, and I didn't like it.

There was a certain dark headed boy named Ike, a little taller than I was, that lived close to where Brian lived. They both rode the same bus I did. One day, Ike and I were talking about Brian being so energetic when he wrestled and played. I said to Ike, "I can't stand him."

Then, Ike replied to me, "He's really playful."

One sunny afternoon during recess, a bunch of us were grouped together playing. I don't remember what we were playing, or exactly what I did to make some of them mad, but I took off running. I was a fast runner and few people could stay up with me, but I felt somebody hitting me in the back. I thought it was Brian, but afterwards I looked back and it was Jason Clark, a boy with short brown hair who was a little taller than I was.

I remember one morning, when Mrs. Elkinson passed out the weekly readers, a magazine that was part of the daily lesson. The headline topic was about John F. Kennedy being sworn in as president of the United States.

As time progressed, it seemed to my nine year old level of thinking like she had turned against me. It seems that the chemistry between us didn't work.

There was a certain thing that happened one day, that in my memory, stands out like a mountain peak, that made it look like she was against me.

She had all of us boys lined up from the front of the room to the back and was giving us words to spell orally. She started on one end and asked each one to spell the word, `Friday.' The first one she asked spelled it wrong. Then she went to the next. I was somewhere in the middle of the line. They spelled that word every way but right.

When it came my turn, she skipped me. The reason she skipped me was the fact that I was a good speller, and she knew that I would spell it right. She went all the way to the other end of the line, and still, no one spelled it right. Then she came back to me. I answered, "f-r-i-d-a-y-."

Then she stiffly responded, "All right," in a low voice. I noticed that she didn't even say whether or not I had spelled it right. For instance, she didn't say, "Well, Robert got it right," or anything. At the time, I had the impression, that she was hoping for someone else to spell it right before she got to me.

There was a boy named Stanley North that lived close to me. He was a year older than I was, and slightly taller. He was also slim with brown hair. One day we were talking about Mrs. Elkinson, I was telling him how I couldn't stand her. To my surprise, he said he liked her. I couldn't understand how anybody could like her. He said to me, "Well, she's mean in a way."

Often times during class, someone would go to the pencil sharpener to sharpen their pencil. But there was something that Mrs. Elkinson would get angry about. She believed that many times, we would break the lead out of our pencil, just for an excuse to go to the pencil sharpener. I remember on one occasion, when she said to a certain boy, "Bring that pencil here." He brought it to her, and she said, "I can tell by looking at this wood right here that you broke the lead out of it with your hand." If we did not admit to it, she would threathen to use a yard stick on us.

One day, I decided to sharpen my pencil. The lead wasn't broke, but it was used to the extent, that I felt like it needed sharpening. When I got to the pencil sharpener, she said to me, "Bring that pencil here." As I was walking toward her desk, I broke the lead out of it with my thumb. I did this because I thought she would get mad if she saw that my pencil still had some lead left.

She asked me angrily, "How'd you break the lead outta this pencil?"

"With my hand," I responded. But she didn't know that it wasn't broken before she called me to her desk.

She interpreted that I was making a confession that I broke the lead out of it, just to go to the pencil sharpener. Then she said sternly to the effect, "Go sharpen it, and don't be breaking it just to go to the pencil sharpener."

Sometime after these things, we had a math test and I failed it. I don't know why I failed it. She showed me the mistakes I made, and it was a mystery to me why I missed them, because when she brought them to my attention I knew the answers. I received an F on my report card. She sent the test papers home with us to have our parents to sign them.

She teased me about getting an F. She said something to the effect, "You need to tell them that an F stands for fine." In retrospect, it seems like she was happier that I got an F than when the time I spelled the word Friday right

But the next day, I forged my parents names on the papers. Also, my parents sent her a note by me demanding an explanation for me getting an F.

When I turned them in, of course she knew the hand writing. She didn't say anything then, but she got in touch with Dorothy, who was in the seventh grade and sent the papers to Mama by her.

That evening when I got off the school bus, I walked through the yard in the evening sunshine, headed to the front door of the house. To my surprise, Mama and Dorothy had the test papers that I had forged her and Daddy's names on, looking at them. She said something to the effect, "So this is why you got an F."

When I went to school the next day, Mrs. Elkinson was angry and talked to me very roughly. She asked me angrily, "Why'd you sign your parents names on those papers?"

I said, "That's the way we done it at Atcooga." (Actually, that wasn't true. I just made up the first excuse I could think of.)

She retorted, "Well, that's not the way we do here!"

She accompanied me to the principal's office. The principal was busy at the time, so we went back to the room.

In a little while, she said to me, "Come with me again, Robert." We went to the principal's office, but again he wasn't ready to see us.

That afternoon, during lunch recess, we were outside playing under the partly cloudy sky. As Mrs. Elkinson was watching us, I saw Mr. Evans come walking up to her and they talked for a while. Then Mr. Evans motioned for me to come to where they where. Mr. Evans took me with him to the office. But he didn't show anger like Mrs. Elkinson did. I stayed up there half the afternoon, and then he asked me, "Whose room is your sister in?"

I replied, Mr. Cottonwood's." Then he went and called her to the office and they reviewed some of my various test papers.

Mrs. Evans was also involved in this conversation. She spoke up in the middle of all this and said in my defence, "Well, that's the best he can do." (Now, Mrs. Evans had a reputation for being soft hearted and easy going. She always defended anybody who got into trouble of any kind. If the school had had an appointed attorney, it would have been her.)

During the process of things, they discovered that except for this one failed test, that I had done good. There before them was a spelling test paper that I had made nearly a hundred on. Mr. Evans replied as he made eye contact with me, "You did good on that."

Then he gave us a lecture about learning our work and doing the right thing. In the course of it he said, "The parents shouldn't get mad at the teacher, they should get mad at that boy right there." Then he sent us back to our rooms, and the whole thing finally smoothed over.

But at the time, regardless of this incident, the relationship between us, in my view, was very bad.

Every encounter that I had with any of the other third grade teachers, was positive. I liked all of them. There was Mrs. Black, a middle aged dark haired lady whose class was next to ours. She seemed very friendly every time I met her or talked to her. A certain dark headed boy named Roger, that I had gotton acquainted with was in her room. I remember visiting her room when I was with Roger.

There was also Mrs. Frazier, a young blonde that seemed very friendly. As I remember seeing her on different occasions, she was slim and rather tall. I can remember wishing that I was in her room.

Then, there was Mrs. Prince. She was an elderly lady with graying hair. I was eating lunch in her room one day. I don't remember the exact details, but I had some kind of a problem getting a coke from the coke machine. Somehow, the coke machine had malfunctioned. As I was eating, she was sitting behind her desk before me. Making eye contact with me in a way that made me feel comfortable, she asked "Did you get you're drink?" I told her that I did.

The other third grade teacher was Mrs. Dangerfield, a middle aged lady with brownish hair. Like the others, it seemed like I would have liked being in her class instead of Mrs. Elkinson's.

I could not understand why I had to be in Mrs. Elkinson's room.

Jesus said, "If a son shall ask bread of any of you that is a father, will he give him a stone? Or if he asks a fish, will he for a fish give him a serpent? Or if he shall ask an egg, will he offer him a scorpion?" (Luke 11:11-12)

God does not give us scorpions. But we must understand that Satan is the God of this present world (11 Cor. 4:4).

In Daniel Chapter Ten, Daniel was waiting for an answer from God concerning a revelation God was showing him. But the message didn't come. The message didn't come because Satan hindered it. God had sent the message by the hand of an angel and Satan had fought with the angel in the atmosphere for twenty-one days, trying to keep him from bringing the message to Daniel. But another angel named Michael came and helped the other angel to overpower Satan.

Because of Satan, life is full of scorpions.

The last half of my third year of school changed the way I felt about school. Through the twisted processes of life, I had been dealt a scorpion.

CHAPTER THREE
REBELLION!

The school year ended, and I was promoted to the fourth grade. The anger in me toward the school played in my mind all summer. I hated school. I trained myself to hate it. I figured out what I was going to do. I decided I was going to burn down the school building.

Now, the Lewis family lived next door to us. There was Mr. Lewis, his wife, and their four daughters. One day, we were playing in our front yard, when I said to Jean, the oldest, "I'm gonna burn the school house down."

Then, she replied disquietly, "Junior, they'll put you in jail..." But her words were meaningless to me.

When school started, there was a boy named Oscar Redmun that I got to be friends with. He was a year older than I was, and also, a grade ahead of me. Being that he lived about a mile from us, we were on the same bus route. After school in the evenings, while we were waiting on the bus (each bus made three trips and we rode the third load), we all gathered at the bus line and marked our places with our school books. Oscar and some of them would be debating and arguing about something that seemed to be of no importance. At first, I didn't know his name, but a certain girl kept calling him Oscar. Because I had never heard the name before, it sounded strange. In the course of all of it, he would say to me, "Com'on Robert, let's go." He gave me the impression that he did not want to argue with them any further. Then, we would go loafing around the school building.

On the bus route, he was one of the first to be picked up, and he always sat on the right front seat. So when I got on the bus I always sat beside of him. Our bus driver's name was Mr. Riggs. He was an average sized man with dark hair.

My teacher's name was Mrs. Rodchester. She was in her earily fifties. I liked her, but it didn't change the way I felt about going to school. I had met her before. When I first enrolled in the school the year before, she came into the office for something. While she was in there, she became involved in the conversation concerning my previous teacher's first name at Atcooga. Mrs. Thomas's first name was Tamka. Apparently, they were puzzled about her name. I took it that they had never heard the name, Tamka before. At the time, I didn't know who Mrs. Rodchester was. She looked at me curiously and we made eye contact. I also remembered her from another occasion. When I was sent to the principal's office the previous year, she came into the office with a complaint. It was concerning the kids running around in an area where they were not supposed to be. It seemed like she was rebuking the principal. She chided with him saying to the effect, "They just keep running in there making a mess out of everything!"

He said to her calmly, "I'll put up a notice."

During the entire year, I don't recall feeling any rebellious feelings toward her. She was a good teacher. She kept things in order and didn't put up with any foolishness.

But here was the irony; although I liked her, I still hated the school. In retrospect, it seems that if I had had her for a teacher when I first came to this school, I never would have rebelled in the way that I was rebelling. But she came into my life a half a year too late. The greatest ambition I had now, was to burn it down.

She was just as tough on misbehavior, and as strict as Mrs. Elkinson. One day, as she (Mrs. Rodchester) sat behind her desk, she showed us five paddles and at least one baby bottle. She used the baby bottle to put on someone's desk when they went to sleep during class.

I remember a certain tall boy named Anderson, who sat on the far back seat. He had red hair. One day, he went to sleep, and slept for a lengthy period of time. Then, he woke up to find a baby bottle sitting beside his head.

She said to him, "Leave that bottle there. Let everybody know you're a baby."

But he, beginning to cry, replied, "But I ain't no baby though."

"Well, you sleep a lot," she responded.

One day, he was acting up, and she made him stand in the hall. After he had been out there for a while, a patrol boy brought him in. (A patrol was a student, usually a sixth or seventh grader, who had been appointed by the principal with the authority to turn someone in if they were doing something wrong. They wore a badge like a policeman.) He informed her that he (Anderson) had a firecracker and was begging for matches so he could shoot it in the hall. He had tried to bum a match from the patrol boy.

She sternly scolded him for having a firecracker in the hall. Then she turned to the class, saying, "He had a firecracker in the hall and was begging for matches to shoot it."

Anderson had a brother named Rodney who was also in the fourth grade. Like Anderson, he was tall with red hair. But his behavior was much better; he was not always getting into mischief. His teacher was a young lady probably in her early thirties with dark hair, named Mrs. Jamison. She happened to come by our class about this time. Then, Mrs. Rodchester shared with her about the firecracker incident. As the two teachers and Anderson stood there in front of the class, Mrs. Rodchester asked Mrs. Jamison, "Now which one would you rather have in your class?"

Then, Mrs. Jamison, making eye contact with Anderson, replied in a tone of voice that suggested that he should be ashamed of himself, "I'd rather have Rodney."

There was a certain boy named Tyler, who sat across the

aisle from me. He had short, dark hair, and was about my height. A boy named Wendell sat behind him.

One afternoon, during geography session, one of the boys sitting next to me, whispered to me, "Wendell's nose is bleeding." I glanced over at him, and saw blood running from his nose, and his eyes were watering.

At first, Mrs. Rodchester was unaware of what was going on. But after the boys kept whispering, she realized something was wrong. Then, she realized something was wrong with Wendell. She asked him, "Wendell, what's the matter?"

He said, "Tyler hit me in the nose."

"Tyler, why'd you do that," she sternly demanded.

He replied, "He kept bothering me with his hands."

Then, after chewing him out, and lecturing about bad behavior, she asked him as she stood in front of the blackboard, "What would you do if someone bloodied someone's nose while you were trying to teach geography?"

He answered, "I donno."

Then, she said to him, "I guess you'd paddle them, wouldn't you?"

He responded something like, "Yeah, I guess."

She said, "Well, that's what I'm gonna do."

Then, she came back to his seat with her paddle and exercised her disciplinary actions as she saw fit.

Now, I was constantly plotting how I was going to set fire to the school house without getting caught. I found a regular sized black pepper can and filled it with gasoline. It fit snuggly in the pocket of my blue jeans.

It just so happened that Oscar did not ride the bus on that particular morning. So I occupied the front seat, sitting next to the aisle where he normally sat. The gas immediately began to leak through the top of the pepper can and subsequently soaked into my leg. It wasn't long before my leg was burning like fire. The bus had to circle the subdivision after I got on. It gradually filled up with kids as it slowly made it's way along the dirt road in the early morning air.

Stanley North, his younger brother, Joey, and his sisters got on the bus after it had made it's way around the subdivision. He was sitting beside me and looked at me curiously, and replied, "I smell gasoline."

Pretending that I smelled nothing, I responded, "I don't."

I had a clip board laying over my pocket where no one would see it. As we were riding down forty-one highway, I noticed a boy named Willie, who had blonde hair sitting directly across the aisle from me looking directly at my wet pants pocket, but he never said anything. Because of the intense burning, I had developed a mental state that I didn't much care if he saw it or not.

The bus patrol was a tall, dark headed boy who was in high school standing right in front of me. He was opening and closing the door as the kids got on. He showed no reaction as to whether or not he smelled the fumes.

When we got to the school house, we started into the door on the south end of the building among the crowds. Then, I heard someone holler, "Mrs. Rodchester's gone to Kentucky."

We had a substitute teacher. She was a slim, young blonde. I had never seen her before, and when this day was over, I never saw her again. After class had begun, I was sitting in my seat, and my leg was still burning from the gasoline. As the fumes continued to infiltrate the air, I finally came to the brilliant conclusion that I was somehow going to have to get this gasoline out of my pocket. The teacher was sitting behind her desk and seemed to be preoccupied with paperwork. The class was quiet while everyone was studying. So I went up and asked her, "Can I go to the bathroom?"

She said to me in a nice, affable tone of voice, "If I let you go to the bathroom, you'll have to stay in at recess for five minutes to make up for it."

Under the circumstances, I thought that was an excellent deal, so I agreed to it. I went into the bathroom, took the can of gasoline out of my pocket, and then, left it setting beside the radiator. I left it there and went back to the room.

The next morning, when we were on the way to school, Oscar whispered to me, "Robert, I think someone's trying to burn down the school building."

I asked him, "How you know?"

He said, "Yesterday, we found a can of gasoline beside the radiator in the bathroom."

I asked, "What'd you do with it?"

He said, "We gave it to Mr. Snyder (the janitor) and he threw it away." I could tell from the tone of his voice, that he had no idea who left it in the bathroom.

One pleasant sunny morning during recess, several of the other boys and I were sitting grouped up at the south end of the front hall, next to where our classrooms were. A certain boy named Allen was standing on top of the concrete steps, and a coke bottle was laying in front of his feet. He was lightly kicking it and it was rolling back and forth. I was afraid he was going to kick too hard and it was going to roll over the steps. Out of the corner of my eye, I saw at least one teacher watching us through the window in the door. Then Allen kicked the bottle over the steps and broke the top off of it.

Mrs. Gravit, the teacher that I had seen watching us, came through the door, scolding us. She was rather tall, slim, and probably in her thirties. As she was scolding everyone concerning the coke bottle, I spoke up and tried to defend what she was saying, because I was afraid of her. As far as I know, she must have misinterpretated what I was saying, and thought that I was trying to be a smart aleck. She started in scolding me as if she thought it was my fault that the bottle was broken. I don't remember the exact words that were exchanged between us, but during the course of it, she slapped me on the leg. On my level of understanding I did not understand why she seemed like she was mad at me because of the bottle. This incident increased my cold war against the school system even the more.

Not every encounter that I had with Mrs. Elkinson was negative. One evening after school, during my fourth year, I paid her a visit at her classroom. It was close to Christmas time. During the course of our little conversation, she showed me her Christmas tree. It was covered with decorations, as it stood near the windows. She talked nice to me then, and I told her that her Christmas tree was pretty.

Since my first plot to set the building on fire fell through, I started plotting another scheme. I cut the top out of a regular sized pet milk can. One morning as we were getting ready for school, I peered out the kitchen window toward the back yard and spied Mama down at the garbage pile. While no one was looking, I got a can of Daddy's lighter fluid and squirted about an eighth of an inch in the bottom of the can.

Since it was too big to put in my pocket, I carried it out in the open. As Pat, Dorothy and I were waiting on the bus, Mama saw me holding the can in my hand. Then, she said to me, "Junior, through that ole tin can down." I put up some excuse that I was taking it to school, then she didn't say anything else.

I got on the school bus with it and sat down beside Oscar as usual. Several of the kids were asking me about the can, and what was in it. I told them it had rain water in it that I had collected in our front yard.

Someone said, "It smells like gasoline."

I explained, "There was gasoline spilt in the yard where the water was at, and that's what makes it smell like gasoline."

Then, Oscar spoke up asking, "Are you taking it for science?"

I replied, "Yeah."

When I got to school, I went into the bathroom with it. As the other boys were starting to pour into the bathroom (I remember the same boy that Mrs. Elkinson scolded the year before among them), no one noticing, I stuffed it down into the trash can among the paper towels and other trash.

Late that afternoon, just before time for our bus to run, most of the kids having already gone home, I walked into the bathroom. When I entered, there was no one except a boy that rode our bus who was just leaving.

I walked over to the garbage can to see if the tin can was still in there. It was still in there among the trash. I got it out and prepared to set the bathroom on fire.

The wall was made out of wood, painted with gray paint. Halfway up, it turned into concrete. I poured the lighter fluid on the wooden part, and as it ran down the wall, I lit a match and set it on fire. Then, I went back outside where everybody else was. Then shortly, the bus came and took everybody home.

The next day, to my disappointment, the school building was still there. There was a black smudge on the wall where the lighter fluid had burned away. The boys all ran their fingers through it.

As Mrs. Rodchester was sitting at her desk, engulfed in her paperwork, I approached her, and said, "Mrs. Rodchester, someone burned a black spot on the wall in the bathroom."

Not even looking up at me, halfway paying me no mind, she said something like, "Okay, that's all right." Then I went on my way, and said nothing more.

There was a certain boy named Derrick Mandell that I met during my fourth year. He was in Mrs. Jamison's room. He was well acquainted with Rodney, Anderson's brother. I noticed him from time to time just standing around in a certain place, instead of playing and running around like the other kids. He was unusual because he would not partake with any activity. He and I became friends. He was about my size and dark headed. His hair was always cut short. I shared with him my plan to burn down the school building. He agreed that the building needed to be burned down, but he was not involved in my attempts to carry it out.

One day, Daddy gave me a brief case that he had run across. I considered it a book satchel. Oscar and my other friends at school, including Derrick told me it was a brief case. We argued and argued whether it was a brief case or a book satchel.

It really never made any difference what we called it, before it was over, I had turned it into a kerosene carrying case. It had sections in it designed to keep some things separated from others. I carried my books in one of the sections, and I don't know how many times I smuggled kerosene to the school, looking for a chance to set it on fire. (I remember being able to buy a peanut butter jar full of kerosene for two cents.)

I liked most of the teachers in this school that I came in contact with. The good experiences that I had with the teachers did not in any way change the way I felt about the school. But there was a certain teacher named Mrs. Dykes, a tall, heavy set lady that enhanced my desire to burn it down.

One sunny day during morning recess, a boy named Jeremy Kennedy, who was a little taller than I was, myself, and two other boys were playing tag. Their names were Jimmy and Tracy. While we were playing, Jimmy and Jeremy had a dispute.

Mrs. Dykes was standing near the curb in front of the grassy lawn. Then, Jeremy complained to her about what Jimmy did to him. She called all four of us there together. Then, she asked me what happened. I started explaining to her what happened between between Jeremy and Jimmy. Then she said to me to the effect, "Okay, you're not involved in this, you stand right out there, indicating with her finger for me to back up about ten feet. Then she asked Tracy what happened. Then, like me, he started to explain what happened between Jimmy and Jeremy. Then she said to him the same thing she said to me. And he backed up out of the way. Then Jeremy started to explain what happened, but then she interrupted him and said in what seemed to be to me, a gripy attitude, "Oh, all of you just sit down on the curb here til the bell rings."

In my view at the time, this teacher had a ridgid personality. She did not seem to have the patience to deal with this little situation. To me, she seemed to be too stiff and gripy to take time to do what was right. To me, it seemed unfair to make us all sit down on the curb. This incident caused more anger and rebellion to rise up in me. But she did not always react in this manner. One day during recess, she approached me, asking me a question concerning our classroom in an affable tone. Somewhere within me I was impressed by her friendly manner at that point.

One night, I got up out of bed while my family were all asleep.

In our house, there was a bar that separated the kitchen and dining room from the living room. There was a gallon jug that had about a quart of gasoline in it that was setting on the shelf in the bar. I was going to swipe some and take it to school. I had a paper coffee cup to put it in. I poured it a little less than half full, then, hid it on a shelf in the closet in my bedroom. In the process of this, I accidently knocked a piece of silverware off the bar. As it rattled on the floor, I rushed as quietly as possible to the bedroom and went back to bed.

The next day, Mama made a comment that she heard a spoon fall in the middle of the night. But nothing else was ever said about it.

The next morning however, I was going to smuggle the gas to school, but the cup was bone dry. The gasoline had evaporated. I learned from this that gasoline evaporates quickly. (Also, the time I spilled the gasoline on my leg, I noticed that it seemed to have dried up rather quickly.)

There is something else that would happen from time to time that would cause the rebellion in me to grow. There were water fountains outside the building in various places. There were occasions when they would all be tore up, and they would stay that way and not be fixed. After school, in the evenings a lot of times, I would be thirsty and would want to go inside the building and get a drink. But the teachers would not let us inside. Once, Stanley North and I devised a plan to sneak to the water fountain. We told the teacher we were going to take a coke bottle inside and put it where it belonged at the coke machine. The water fountain was just down the hall. As we started toward the water fountain, I could hear her shoes tapping the hardwood floor as she was making the turn from the front entrance to check on us. Then, she sternly sent us outside.

There was a fifth grade teacher named Mr. Mason. I did not know him very well, but he had a reputation for being easy to get along with. One evening after school, I approached him behind the back hall and asked him, "Mr. Mason, can I go in and get a drink?"

He answered favorably and replied, "Yeah, I'm a little dry myself." Then we both went in and got a drink. I was impressed with how easy he was to get along with.

My fourth year finally came to an end, and I was promoted to the fifth grade. My fifth grade teacher's name was Mrs. Currie, a middle aged lady with gray hair. She was very different from the other teachers in some ways. She did not believe in paddlings. She believed in other forms of discipline.

I liked her as I did Mrs. Rodchester. Although she didn't believe in paddlings, she had ways of discipline that would make me mad a lot of times. But there is nothing that she did that would have enhanced my desire to burn down the school. If anything, she would have diverted my attention to much better things, if she had come into my life a year and a half earlier.

But there was another problem. After the adverse experiences I had already had, healthy discipline would cause me to rebel. Mrs. Currie's disciplinary actions were good, but sometimes I would take it in a negative way. For instance, I once disagreed with her about something on my test paper. She would correct me for getting mad. My story would be that I wasn't mad, I was disgusted. Then I would be mad because she said I was mad.

This year, Derrick Mandell and I were in the same room. We were planning to sit next to each other. I sat down in one desk, and said, "I'll sit in this desk and you sit in this one." When I said this, he stood, gazing at me with a smile.

But what we didn't know was, that Mrs. Currie seated everybody alphabetically. But our names were next to each other alphabetically, so we ended up sitting next to each other after all.

One sunny day, as recess ended, we all came into the room. A boy with light brown hair who was slightly taller than I was, named Jay Hughes that sat on the front row, was laughing about an incident that just occurred. We were seated in our seats waiting for Mrs. Currie to come into the room. But some of the other boys in the class were not there. The story was, that several of the boys had been across the boundary during recess. They had been in an area that was forbidden ground because it would disturb other classes. There was a parking area close to the seventh grade rooms, and they had been playing and running among the parked cars. Mr. Todd, a seventh grade teacher about six feet tall, medium built, with thick glasses and brown hair came out of the classroom and hollered at them. Some of them got caught and some got away. He took them inside. Jay was bragging and laughing because he and some of the others got away. For some reason, Mrs. Currie delayed to come into the room. "Mrs. Currie's gonna come in and ask, `Where's the boys?' then we'll tell her that they got caught down there. I'm glad I got away," he chortled.

But the picnic was short lived. After a little while, there came the boys filing in from down the hall, but Mrs. Currie was with them. Then the laughter was over. It was payday. She immediately took the names of all the ones who were involved in this thing. Then she sternly lectured them about what they had done. She informed them that they would be disciplined by staying in at recess for a lengthy period of time.

On one occasion, I was smuggling a container of some sort filled with kerosene in my brief case. Late that afternoon as we were waiting for our buses in the auditorium (Now, early in the morning before school, and after school in the evenings, if it was raining or too cold to go outside, everyone had to wait in the auditorium for their buses. Whenever the teacher that was in charge (usually Mr. Todd or Mr. Prince, a fifth grade teacher who was tall and heavy set with dark hair) had something to say, he would blow the whistle to get everybody quiet. When one of the buses came, he would blow the whistle and announce which bus was there. One day, Mr. Prince blew the whistle and exclaimed, "Over to the sides," because too many people were on the floor. (Now, the Mrs. Prince who taught the third grade was his wife.) But everyone misunderstood him. We thought he said, outside. Then several hundred people flooded the floor and headed outside. Then he had to run everyone of us down to get us back in the building. I remember his gruff voice retorting, "I outta take my belt of to every one of you"), I told Derrick that I had kerosene in my briefcase. Then, he started playing like he was going to tell everybody that I had kerosene. He started hollering in a whispering voice, "Robert's got kerosene."

I was afraid someone would hear him, and I whispered to him, "Don't do that, somebody might hear you."

There were occasions when Mrs. Currie would be absent from school and we would have a substitute teacher.

On one such occasion, a certain substitute named, Mrs. Keene, a middle aged lady with dark hair was filling in.

There was a certain ball field on the south side of the elementary building that our room always played baseball in, during recess. It was beside the highway. (In the western section of this area was the primary building were the first and second grades were.) Sometimes, the ball would get knocked across the highway and whichever teacher was available would have to go across the highway to retrieve it. The students were never allowed to cross the highway. One sunny day, a certain boy named Gene came up to Mrs. Dykes and said, "Mrs. Dykes, our ball's across the road." I was standing close by, and I remember him making eye contact with me as he was talking to her. As I returned his gaze, a grin broke across his face.

At the time, they were repaving the highway, and she responded stiffly, "Well, I ain't gonna get tar all over my shoes going over there to get it."

Then, he asked, "Can I go over there and get it?"

"No, you can't," she stiffly responded.

A little later, I saw him talking to Mrs. Todd, a fifth grade teacher who was probably in her thirties. (She was the wife of Mr. Todd, the seventh grade teacher that the boys in our class had gotten into trouble with.) Dressed in her lengthy white dress, she was bent over talking to him in a kind way. Then, she crossed the highway and retrived it.

On this particular warm, sunny day that Mrs. Keene was filling in, as recess had begun, the boys in our room went to the area to play ball as always. (I never did play with them. Myself and some of the others always stood behind the chain link fence and watched.) As they were beginning to start the game, the boys from Mrs. Rodchester's fourth grade class came up to them and informed them that the ball field was their's. The boys in our class thought they were being invaded and they all got into an argument over the field.

Now, the story was that Mrs. Rodchester had decided that our room should share the ball field with her class. But the problem was, that nobody had explained that to our class. So everybody was confused and was arguing about it. All the boys were saying to each other, "It's our's."

The other's were saying, "No, it's our's."

Then, Mrs. Rodchester came to the scene and angrily sent our class back to the room. I remember being puzzled as everyone was going inside. When we all were in the room, seated in our seats, she came into the room and scolded everybody about sharing the ball field. She ordered everyone to get out their daily assignments and get to work.

Somewhere in the course of this, some of the girls in the

class came up to the window and asked what we were doing in the room. Some of the boys were explaining to them about what had happened. I remember the girls looking up through the windows with a curious expression on their faces, talking to them.

After Mrs. Rodchester left the room, some of the boys got a beach ball and started throwing it around the room.

DIAGRAM 2
CAMPUS LAYOUT

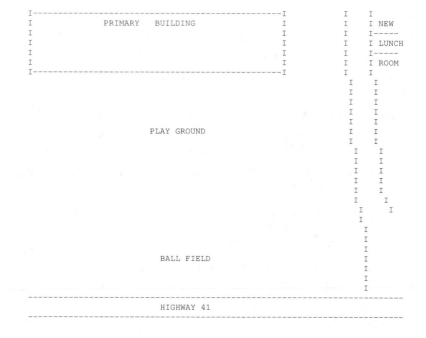

In a few minutes, she came back to the room to check on us. As she was standing in the doorway, the ball was laying in the aisle on the hardwood floor. One of the boys informed her that while she was gone, some of the boys were playing ball.

She asked, "Who threw the ball?"

"Randy," one of the other boys replied.

Then, she said to him, "Randy, get up and go to the office."

Then Randy, who was tall and slim with brown hair, got out of his seat and started toward the door to go to the office.

Then she stopped him and said to the effect, "No, just sit down." Then, she told everybody to get back to work again.

Later that afternoon, Mr. Evans came to visit our class. When he walked into the room, one of the boys was standing by his desk reading aloud, as the teacher had directed. Mr. Evans stood before the class and said to him, "Sit down." He was carrying a paddle with him and he was very angry. He stood before the class and hotly scolded all of us for not sharing the ball field. He said something to the effect, "I like little boys and girls, but I don't like boys who do not share." Then, he threateningly took about two steps toward one of the boys on the front row, and asked him angrily, "Do you think it's funny?"

The boy responded, "No, I don't think it's funny."

Anger and rebellion was building up in me against him and against the school system because of this thing. I remember feeling so angry at him that I was planning to stab him if he had attempted to paddle us. However, most of the encounters I had with this principal were positive. Most of the time, I liked him. This was an outstanding incident. I felt that it was unfair for our class to be punished over this issue, because we were not informed in advance that Mrs. Rodchester's class wanted to play ball in that particular area. As a result, anger and rebellion arose in me.

I guess because I liked Mrs Rodchester, when I was in her room the year before, my rebellion was not directed at her near as much as it was Mr. Evans. There were occasions when she filled in as a substitute teacher in our (Mrs. Currie's) class. I remember once when she was quizzing our class on the subject of history. As she sat behind the desk, she was asking who invented various things such as light bulbs, telephones, or other inventions. Then she asked, "Who invented the television?"

Everyone quietly conveyed that they didn't know.

Then she giggled as her dark brown hair dangled around her face, and confessed, "I don't either."

There were occasions when we would bring our lunch to school, instead of eating in the lunch room. When the kids that ate in the lunch room went to eat, the ones from several classes who brought their lunch would meet in a certain classroom to eat. It wouldn't be the same room all the time, but they would skip around. When we finished eating, we would go outside to recess. I remember once when we went to Mrs. Todd's room. She seemed nice to everyone as far as I knew. As we were eating lunch, I happened to be sitting on the front seat. Then, she asked me, "What's your name?"

I replied, "Robert Massingill."

One thing about her I remembered well. She could use a typewriter. One day, when we were sent to her room for a special assignment, she had borrowed one from the office, and was doing some typing. Her fingers seemed to be going ninety miles an hour. To all of our amazement, she wasn't even looking at the typewriter. She gazed around the room and smiled at everyone as she typed.

One day, when I brought my lunch, we were told that the ones who brought their lunch would go to Mrs. Dykes's room. I went to her room and ate lunch as always. Then I went outside to recess as always. While I was out on the playground, a certain boy hollered at me and said, "Robert, Mrs. Dykes wants you."

I went to the room where she was, and she asked me to the effect, "Did you tell me that you were through eating, and was going outside?"

I answered, "No." This was because I didn't know that I was supposed to tell her; none of the other teachers had ever mentioned it. I assumed that she knew that.

She said, "Go sit down. You'll have to stay in till recess is over because you didn't let me know you were going out."

It seemed that this was unfair to me, and like many other occasions, it caused the rebellion in me toward the school to grow.

For the most part, I wouldn't tell anyone how I felt about the school system and the adverse way they seemed to be operating in sometimes. Once in a while, I would get excessively angry about something and say to someone that I was going to burn the school house down. On one such occasion, I was in an angry attitude, and I said to Lance Darrow, a boy that I had recently befriended that I was going to burn the school house down. Two other boys that we were both acquainted with were standing there when I said it. One's name was Frankie, a slim, brown headed boy, and the other was a boy named Shawn who had blonde hair. They both were about my size.

Lance was a grade or two behind me, and he and Shawn were in the same room. A lot of times, Shawn and I would wrestle around. I did not put out much energy when I wrestled with him. I would pretend that I was going to let him beat me up. One morning, he ran up to me and put his hand on my shoulder and playfully asked, "Are you gonna let me beat you up again today?"

After I had made the comment, Shawn said to the effect, "He's gonna get in trouble."

Lance said to him, "Don't tell nobody about that, he was just joking."

Later, Frankie asked me, "When are you gonna do it?"

I said something to him to the effect that I didn't know.

There was a certain boy named Trevor who was probably about a year younger that I was who lived on the same bus route I did. He was about my height with light colored hair. He also had two older sisters. There was something about him that stood out like a mountain peak in my memory. He was always exceptionally nice to everyone. I don't remember him ever saying anything bad about anyone, or saying anything unkind to anyone. I remember once when he had a friendly dispute with another boy over the bus line. The other boy whose name was Roger accused him of scrouging in front of him. But Trevor insisted that he had the space marked with his books. He said to Roger in a firm, polite manner, "Now, I got here fair and square."

Finally, becoming convinced that Trevor was telling it straight, Roger asked, "Well, when did you get here?" Then, Trevor explained it to him to where he understood.

One morning before school, Trevor and I were hanging around one of the basketball goals that were placed in various areas over the playground. I shared with him my feelings about Mr. Evans and about my plan to stab him. Then, he began to say to me in a joking manner, "Oh, Robert, please don't beat Mr. Evans up." But there was no one else that I mentioned it to.

On a certain occasion, Mrs. Currie had brought a certain musical instrument to the school to show to us. As I remember the incident, she called it an organ. Then, she developed a habit of leaving it in the room overnight. As I was plotting to burn down the school building, the thought of her organ being in the building cut at my conscience, and I thought to myself, *"Mrs. Currie's organ!"* I couldn't stand the thought of burning up her organ. I felt terrible. The thought of it hurt me inside. If there was any reason for me not to try to burn down the school, it would have been the fact that her organ was in the building.

I was experimenting with every flammable liquid that I could get my hands on. I found some linseed oil that Daddy had brought home from work. I found an old snuff box, filled it full, and smuggled it to school.

One day, as we were in the lunch line, all the other boys were talking about smelling paint. They thought there was some painting going on nearby. Everyone was smelling paint but me. I remember asking someone to the effect, if they smelled paint. One of them answered, "Yeah, I smell paint." But they didn't seem to be paying any attention to the fact that there was no painting going on anywhere.

But on this occasion, like many others, I never did get a chance to set the building on fire.

Lance Darrow and I had become close friends. But other than the time when I told him and the other two that I was going to burn down the school building, I never told him anything else about it.

There was a boy named Leon Garrett that started coming to our school. The first time I recall seeing him was when the school bus pulled across the railroad tracks at a certain intersection. Then several kids came running up toward the front of the bus. Being in the lead, he seemed to have a defiant expression on his face. Lance, sitting beside me in the same seat whispered to me saying something like, "That boy used to be a boxing champion at Crown School." Somehow in the process of things he became friends with Lance and I. Both of them had neatly trimmed brown hair and all three of us were about the same size. The three of us hung out together a lot. At the same time, I still hung around Derrick Mandell. But he did not run around with the rest of us, so I associated with him during intervals.

One morning before school, Lance and I were walking up the sidewalk on the north end of the building. A boy named Chris was walking behind us. I saw Mrs. Elkinson standing on top of the steps of the north end of the front hall looking in our direction. I don't know if she was watching us or not, but I was keeping an eye on her as if I were walking through a jungle, spying on a wild cat about to attack.

About that time, Joey North ran up from behind us, and ran in between Lance and I. He was just playing around, acting silly. He turned around and started to head back the other way, but ran into Chris and they bumped heads. Both of them busted out crying.

Mrs. Elkinson, who saw the whole thing immediately came storming off the steps, and down to where we were. She asked them to the effect, whether or not they were all right. (They each had a knot on their forehead.)

Then, I tried to explain to her what happened. I said to her, "It was an accident."

Then, she scowled at me in a stormy attitude and exclaimed, "Maybe you did it, let's see and find out!"

Then, Lance explained to her what happened. Then, she halfway calmed down, looked at me with a hateful expression on her face, and said nothing.

This incident did nothing, but add fuel to the flames of rebellion that were already blazing within me.

CHAPTER FOUR
DIVINE INTERVENTION

"A soft answer turns away wrath: but grievous words stir up anger" (Proverbs 15:1).

Sometimes, a soft answer comes too late. Sometimes, grievous words get to the spiritual crime scene far ahead of the soft answer, and do devastating damage. Sometimes, the damage is beyond human repair.

Ephesians, Chapter Six, Verse Four says, "Children, obey your parents in The Lord: for this is right. Verse Four says, "And, ye fathers, provoke not your children to wrath: but bring them up in the nurture and admonition of The Lord."

Verse One could be translated, "Children, obey your school teachers in The Lord." Verse Four could be translated, "School teachers, provoke not your students to anger."

Children are supposed to obey their school teachers in The Lord. But what good does it do to pound on the table with Verse One, and then ignore Verse Four? Probably none. But it could do a lot of harm.

First Chronicles 21:1 says, "And Satan stood up against Israel and provoked David to number Israel." A certain evangelist said once concerning this scripture, "You'll do things when you're provoked that you won't do any other time. When you're angry or upset." Somehow in the twisted process of things, I was provoked into anger in the last half of my third year of school. Then, there were other provocations that compounded the anger.

Can the pieces of a shattered life be put back together again? In the thirty-seventh chapter of Ezekiel, Ezekiel was carried away in The Spirit, and was set down in a valley that was full of bones. The bones were scattered everywhere. In Verse Three, God asked Ezekiel, "Can these bones live?"

And Ezekiel looked around at the devastated sight before him, and said, "O Lord God, thou knowest."

Ezekiel wasn't sure about this. He didn't know if they could live or not. With human effort, they couldn't.

Can someone spiritually live after their life is shattered, and the pieces scattered into the wind?

It seems, that after my third year of school, my emotional school life was shattered, and the pieces scattered in all directions.

In Verses Four and Five, God said to Ezekiel, "Prophesy upon these bones, and say unto them, `O ye dry bones, hear The Word of The Lord. Thus saith The Lord God unto these bones; Behold, I will cause breath to enter into you, and ye shall live."

Do you remember the T.V. series, ,Dragnet ? You remember how Sergeant Friday narrated the preface of the show? He would say something like, "This is the city, Los Angeles California. Everyday life goes on here. People go about their daily routine. They go to work and back, or they go shopping, and all their other activities. But sometimes, criminals interrupt everyday life and things get out of hand. That's when I go to work. I carry a badge."

The same could be said in the everyday lives of thousands of young children. Everyday, thousands of children go to school as a normal routine. For the most part, the children go to school to learn. They make friends. Usually, they make friends with their teachers.

But sometimes, things go foul. Sometimes, things get twisted up in the life of a young child, and go unnoticed. At face value, it looks like everything is fine. But under the surface, devastating, unrepairable damage is done. There is nothing any human can do to change it. It spins out of human control. Depending on the makeup of the child, and the choices he or she makes, sometimes, criminals, such as bank robbers or serial killers may be produced from such twisted childhood experiences.

As The Holy Spirit of God moves in the Earth, God looks down from heaven, and says, "That's when I go to work."

I had now been promoted to the sixth grade. My school teacher was Mr. Bradshaw, a tall, slim man in his mid fifties. He was the first male teacher I ever had. Like most of the other teachers before him, I liked him, but also like most of the others, he came into my life a little late. Also, like most of the other teachers before him, I got a little mad at him occasionally.

The first day that we met him, he sat behind his desk, and said to us apologetically to the effect, "I hate to tell you this, but there's the books that you're gonna have to use." He was referring to the stack of ragged books stacked on a table behind us.

I remember once, when he was lecturing the class about the importance of getting an education. In the course of it, he said, "If you don't get an education, you'll be digging ditches."

When he said that, a boy named Kirby who who sat behind me said to me, "That'd be fun wouldn't it Robert?"

I looked around at him, grinning, "Yeah, it would."

Once, he said to us, "The first whipping I ever got was with a hickory switch. Another boy put me up to shooting a spit wad at the girls. Then, I got a good switching. I never got another one."

I remember a certain girl named Wanda, that sat on the back seat about two aisles over from me. (I sat next to the back seat.) She was tall with long brown hair, and to me, she acted comical. Some of the boys sitting close to her would aggravate her, and she would slap at them in a way that tickled me when I watched her. She was a little older than the rest of us. Apparently, she had failed a grade or two. One of the boys who aggravated her was Kirby. Like Wanda, he was a little older than the rest of us. He was a little bigger than I was, with short brown hair.

One day, Mr. Bradshaw had started english session. I was sitting there about halfway day dreaming, when all at once, he raised his voice and said, "All right, everybody that ain't got it, line up right over here!," indicating with his finger, his right hand side of the room. He was referring to the previous daily homework assignment.

I had several pages of homework that I had done the night before. As ninety-five percent of the class lined up, myself, and about four other people stayed in our seats. I said aloud, "I've got it right here."

Some of the other boys were gazing at me in amazement because they couldn't believe that I had it prepared.

I remember Wanda standing at the back of the line. She turned around and looked at all of us. Then she shrugged her shoulders, as she gave us her usual comical grin.

As far as I remember, Mr. Bradshaw made a note of the ones of us who had the assignment. But for some reason, he didn't take them up or double check to make sure that we actually had it. This was not really unusual, as there were many times that he didn't ask us to turn in certain assignments. Then, he said to the ones lined up, "You can either stay in at recess and do this assignment, or take a paddling." I remember everyone quickly heading for their seats.

During lunch break that day, some of us were in the room talking. Wanda said to us, "If he was gonna paddle us, I was gonna go through that winder back there."

But what was really funny, was that afterwards, I got to checking, and discovered that I didn't even have the assignment.

One day during lunch, two boys named Jasper, and Jesse, Wanda, and myself were in the room by ourselves. Everyone else was either in the lunch room, or outside. Suddenly, Jasper and Jesse playfully grabbed me and was going to put me on the operating table. (In the back of the room, there were some cabnets, and some other pieces of houseware. Among them was a table with a white top.) Although they both were bigger than I was, it was a half a days work for both of them to get me up there. They both were tall and lanky. Jasper had dark brown hair, but Jesse was blonde headed. We were rolling and scuffling, and I remember a layer of dust we rolled through in the process. Wanda was laughing at us, but she seemed concerned that someone would see us and tell Mr. Bradshaw on us. For all we knew, someone could easily see us through the window, or just look in the room. She kept saying to us, "Somebody might tell on you'all." She said this over and over.

Later that afternoon, we were in the middle of class, and were having class discussion. If anyone had anything to say, pertaining to the lesson, they would raise their hand. Different people were raising their hands and giving their input as they received permission. Then, Wanda raised her hand. Mr. Bradshaw gave her permission to speak. Then, she said something like, "Mr. Bradshaw, during lunch today, Jasper and Jesse grabbed that boy and they wrestled all over the floor."

I noticed that although she knew my name just as she knew their's, she didn't call my name. She referred to me as `that boy.'

Mr. Bradshaw gave me a halfway glare, and then he said, "I'll tell you what I'm gonna do. From now on, the ones of you that don't go to lunch will stay in your seats. If anybody gets outta their seats, or talks too loud, they'll get a paddling."

Someone was always assigned to take names of anybody who got out of their seats or talked loud. We were under this restriction for the rest of the year.

But what was so funny, and it tickled me every time I thought about it, was the fact that Wanda was so worried that someone might tell on us.

One sunny day, while we were in class, it was suddenly reported that President John F. Kennedy had just been shot. A certain girl with long blonde hair, who was sitting in front of me at the time, turned around and exclaimed to me, "Mrs. Kennedy too!"

I remember during recess, that a certain tall boy, with dark brown hair, who was in one of the other sixth grade classes, proclaiming in the hall, "Kennedy got shot with a shotgun!"

Now, the plot to burn down the school was still playing it's hand in the dark corners of my mind. I had a habit of carrying loose matches in my pocket. One day, I moved a certain way in my seat during class, and two of the matches rubbed heads and struck in my pocket. I felt it burn my leg for a second, then there was a smoky smell all in the room.

There was a certain boy named Brad in our class that had a reputation for sneaking around smoking cigarettes. Everyone was looking around the room trying to figure out where the smell was coming from. They started making jokes that Brad was hiding in there somewhere, smoking (Brad wasn't there at the time). They opened a cabinet in the back of the room and hollered, "Are you in there Brad?"

There had been various occasions when some of the boys got caught smoking and were punished. Mr. Bradshaw used to give us lectures about smoking, telling us that it was bad and we shouldn't do it. He asked us a question one day, "You know why people start smoking?"

Some of the boys asked, "Why?"

"Because it looks big," he replied in a halfway grin.

On the north end of the playground, there was a certain unpainted block building that looked like some kind of a shop. We were never allowed inside of it. But one day during recess, Mr. Bradshaw was in there talking to someone. Some of the boys were giggling, and saying that he was smoking. I remember peeking through the window, and sure enough, there he stood with his foot propped up on a table with a cigarette between his fingers. Actually, he never told us that he didn't smoke, he just told us not to.

But something happened during my sixth year that for a while, took away my desire to burn down the school, or to do any violence against anyone.

One day, we were all called into the auditorium. As far as I remember the whole elementary school was there. There was a man there giving a lecture about God and His Son, Jesus. I had heard about God and Jesus and The Holy Ghost throughout my childhood life, but not in the way that I was about to hear it now.

From the earliest memories that I have in my life, there was a man named *H.H. Ezzard, that owned, and run a store on highway forty-one, south of Dalton. He was well acquainted with my parents, and we traded with them all the time. He was a Christian man and talked to me about God all the time. He always told me about the Ten Commandments, and the difference between right and wrong. I suppose that one of the ironies to this story was that years before, he had played a major part in having this school built, and as much as I thought of him, I was trying to burn it down.

These were the days before prayer was taken out of school. We always had prayer in school, and The Bible was taught. I remember especially in the fourth grade, how Mrs. Rodchester shared with us from The Bible the story of Jesus's ministry on Earth. He had twelve disciples, and one of them betrayed him, and turned him over to the high priest. She also explained to us how they crucified Him and killed Him. I didn't like it because they killed Him. This seemed wrong and unfair. Then she shared with us how He rose from the dead. I liked that part. It sounded better.

Also, in my fifth year, Mrs. Currie taught us about Jesus. I remember her sharing with us about the time that Peter, James, and John went to sleep when Jesus was praying in the garden of Gethsemane. I remember her teaching us how the soldiers that came and arrested Him all fell backwards to the ground. And also she told us about Peter cutting off a man's ear with the sword.

But the message I was now about to hear was different. Up

until now, I had heard of a historical Jesus. I had heard of a God who was far away and spoke to people in ancient Bible days. I had never heard of the born again experience, until now. Until now, I had never understood about being saved by asking Jesus for forgiveness for sins.

This man's name was *George Eaker. He was from Valdosta Georgia. The dark haired man, who appeared to be in his thirties, stood before us, proclaiming to us how Jesus would accept us into the family of God.

He gave everyone a certain form to fill out and send in, if we wanted to take Bible lessons through the mail.

A little dark headed boy named Trent who sat in front of me, said to me, "I'm gonna fill that out and send it in."

As far as I remember, I said, "I am too."

So I filled it out and sent it in. During the process of this, I learned how to get saved. In my bedroom alone, I asked Jesus to save me. I remember feeling a supernatural joy in me during this time.

Stanley and Joey North lived up the road from us and I shared this with them. They understood what I was talking about, because they had a baptist background, and went to church sometimes.

During this time, I don't remember having any thoughts about burning down the school. For the time being, I was delivered from the dark side.

CHAPTER FIVE
RETURN OF THE SKELETON

I don't remember exactly how long I held on to my faith in God, or how long I took the Bible lessons. But after a while, I gradually slipped back to where I was before.

I have always believed that when a person has a supernatural encounter with God, they are never the same again. They may backslide and go do all the mean things they did before. They may turn their back on God completely. They may be better off or they may be worse off. After the experience I had with God, when I was in the sixth grade, somewhere deep within me, God had left His supernatural mark.

I was now promoted to the seventh grade. I was in Mrs. Collins's homeroom at first, but in a short time, I was moved to Mr. Todd's room. I had already met some of the seventh grade teachers before. There had been occasions that I had had friendly encounters with Mrs. Collins, a fairly young, tall lady who had medium length brown hair. I remember a comical encounter that Jeremy Kennedy had with her on a sunny afternoon after school. On the north section of the school playground, there was a small store where they sold candy and ice cream. When it was closed, they kept it pad locked. This particular afternoon, Jeremy, myself, and a big heavy set, sandy headed boy, who was a patrol were gathered there talking. I never knew the patrol boy's name, but he acted in a goofy like way that seemed comical. Jeremy was sitting on the ground under the pad lock. As we were casually talking, he ran his hand up the side of the door and touched the lock with his fingers. When he did this, the patrol said to him, "I'm gonna have to take you in for that."

Jeremy said something like, "No, I'm not gonna go with you." They argued around about it for a while. Finally, the patrol wrestled him to the front of the building where Mrs. Collins, and another teacher who taught the seventh grade at the time, named Mr. Bradley, a medium sized man with dark hair were standing.

Then, the patrol boy said to Jeremy, "Tell'em what you done."

"No, you tell'em," Jeremy argued.

The patrol said, "You tell'em." They debated on who should be the one to tell them what he did, as the two teachers curiously looked on to see what would happen next.

Finally, Jeremy said to them, "You know that lock on the store? I was running my hand up the wall and I touched it."

As Mrs. Collins gazed at the patrol, tittering, she replied, "You silly thing." Then, for the most part they laughed the whole thing off.

But Mr. Bradley spoke up and presented a hypothetical situation. He replied something to the effect, "Well, touching the lock didn't hurt nothing, but let's suppose someone were to break into it tonight and steal a bunch of stuff. Then the law investigates and finds your fingerprints on it. Then there you'd be." But touching the lock was no big deal to the two teachers.

One snowy evening when I was in the fourth grade, I had gotten permission to help call buses. The way it worked was, that one or two students stood at the front entrance and when a bus approached, they would go inside and tell the teacher in charge of the floor which bus was coming. Mrs. Rodchester walked up and asked me what I was doing, and I told her. Then she replied sharply, "Well, you're a super-duper to call buses. Get your boggen on."

As the large snow flakes heavily blanketed the school yard and landscape, our bus being one of the last to run, delayed it's arrival. As Mrs. Collins and I stood on the porch, she said to me,

"I don't think it's coming, do you?"

I answered, "I donno."

The seventh grade changed classes, so I was in all the teacher's rooms. Mr. Todd taught math. Mrs. Collins taught history. Mrs. Hayes taught science. Everyone said that Mrs. Hayes looked like Samantha on ,Bewitched. Mrs. Cooper taught english, and Mr. Prince, no longer teaching the fifth grade, taught spelling.

Mr. Prince was a good teacher and easy to get along with, as long as a person followed the rules and did right. I remember once, when a certain boy whose name was Devera and who was about an inch taller than I was with short brown hair, did not do his homework assignment. Mr. Prince called him up front and stood him before him. Then, he slowly turned him around and around and pretended to be examining his head like a doctor. Then, he said, "I don't see anything wrong with your head. There's no reason for you not to have your homework." At least he had a sense of humor. Then, he sent the boy back to his seat.

He (Mr. Prince) did not teach this class very long. We had at least three other teachers who came and went throughout the year.

Before school in the mornings, and after school in the afternoons, boys ran in packs like timber wolves. Lance Darrow had moved away and was going to another school. Leon Garrett and I continued to be friends. There was a boy named Bert Anderson that we befriended. He, Leon, and I sat next to each other in Mr. Todd's homeroom class.

There was a boy named Jody Coltrane who started coming to our school. He acted meaner than he really was, and he and Leon were somewhat rivals. I don't remember what started it, but they got into a fight one morning. Words were exchanged between them. Then they started slapping around at each other, but it never amounted to much. After they had stopped slapping at each other, Leon and another boy began to argue.

The other boy replied sarcasticly, "Your lips bleeding."

To which Leon retorted, "My lip ain't bleeding." His lip wasn't bleeding. But I noticed around his gums that there was a small trace of blood.

Sometime later, I went into the class room after the afternoon recess, and a certain boy said to Leon, "You got'im then." The story was, that unknown to me, there had been a fight between Leon and Jody, and Leon got him on the ground and got the best of him.

Jody and I also got acquainted and associated with each other somewhat, but none of them knew about my plot to burn down the school.

One morning before school, Jody, myself, and a host of other boys, Leon included, were ganged up in an alley behind the south end of the the front hall. (It wasn't really an alley. It was the area between the front and back halls.) Jody had a letter that his girlfriend had written him. He handed it to me and told me to read it to myself. He would not let any of the others see it. I stood behind him in the alley, reading it in the brisk morning air. The others were saying to him, "Ah, come on Coltrane, let us read it."

But he would not. Being a little bigger than the rest of the boys, he held them at bay. "Stand back!," he damanded.

I stood and read it while he fussed and argued with the crowd. Out of the corner of my eye, I remember seeing Leon looking up at him, with a defiant stance.

He told me not to tell anyone what it said, so I did not. Leon and Bert nagged at me all day to tell them what was in the letter, but I would not tell them. I told Jody I wouldn't tell anybody, and I kept my word.

During the afternoon recess, the two of them ganged up on me, and was going to force me to tell them what the note said. We were at the south end of the back hall when it started. We rolled and wrestled all over the ground. I had my arms around Bert's legs, and he fell onto the ground. Leon hollered at Bert, and said, "Grab his legs!"

Bert hollered, "He's got my legs!" Finally, I wrestled away from them and ran toward the north end of the building. As I approached the north end, I looked back, and saw them standing in the afternoon sunlight looking at me from where they were standing. Then I turned around the end of the building and vanished out of their sight. (It wasn't unusual for Leon and I to have a wrestling match. I remember once in Mrs. Robinson's spelling class when we were wrestling in the floor. I remember seeing her white shoes rapidly tapping across the floor to break us up.)

What was sort of funny, was that later that day during class, Leon said to me, "Robert, please tell us what it said."

But I said, "No, I ain't telling anybody what it said."

One day as I was climbing the stairs on the back hall, headed to my classroom, a familiar boy met me at the top of the stairs. He said to me something like, "Hey Robert, how're you doing?"

Being caught off guard, I asked him, "Are you Lance Darrow?"

He responded to my dumb question saying, "Yeah, it's me." I was glad to see him and we talked in the hall. But after the seventh grade, I don't remember ever seeing him anymore.

There was a boy in our homeroom class named, Richard Rose. He was at least six feet tall, slim, and had brown hair. He, Bobby, Bert, and myself were all friends. If Richard got mad, he was high tempered. He was also defiant against the teachers if they tried to discipline him in some way that he disagreed with. I remember a couple of times that he had a run-in with Mrs. Hayes. Once, she stepped out of the room for a few minutes. When she returned, he was out of his seat. She asked him sternly, "What're you doing outta your seat?"

"I was throwing a piece of paper away," he replied.

She said to him, "You're not suppose to be outta your seat. You stay in at recess, young man."

He retorted something to the effect, "I ain't staying in at recess!"

Then, they argued and disputed about it. As we were leaving class, I heard him tell someone that he was not going to stay in.

There was one occasion when she was teaching on the subject of different kinds of vitamins that were healthy for various parts of the human body. She asked the class the question, "Why are carrots good for your eyes?"

I remember him speaking up boldly from the back of the class, "Because you don't ever see a rabbit wearing glasses."

No one laughed when he made his comment. She didn't make any comment, but from the expression on her face, I could tell that she didn't appreciate his answer.

One day, she had been out of the room for something. Then, she came in and corrected several different people for misbehaving. She said to Richard, "You can stay in at recess for that little demonstration you did."

He retorted in a defiant attitude, "I didn't do no demonstration!"

They argued about it, but I don't remember whatever happened.

One sunny day, Richard and I were playing marbles. Somehow in the process of things, we lost a marble. Jody Coltrane was standing nearby. As we were looking for the marble under the shade of a nearby tree, he stood there, looking innocent. I figured he was standing on it. Then Richard grinned at him and said, "All right, Coltrane."

Then Jody grinned and moved his foot, and there it was under his tennis shoe.

One morning when we arrived at school, we went into the auditorium, and there was a certain section of the bleachers that no one was sitting on. The story was, that just before we got there, someone had set the building on fire under the bleachers. They had put the fire out, but no one was sitting in that section.

I don't know the details, but someone said that they caught the ones involved in setting the fire.

It was told that during the ordeal, the kids were rolling in the floor laughing about it. That morning in Mrs. Collins's class, she was lecturing to us that it wasn't funny. She said to us, "We wouldn't have anywhere to go to school, but this ole yellow school up here, (referring to Atcooga) and it wouldn't hold half of us."

I plotted several schemes, trying to set the school house on fire. For instance, I took a gas cylinder to school one day, and hid it behind the radiator. (A gas cylinder that I am referring to is the kind that goes in a B.B. gun.) The plan was for it to get hot and explode. A certain boy who had red hair, named Aaron found it. He said to me, "Look what I found." We talked and laughed about it. Then he took it home with him.

He came back the next day and said to me, "I took the cap off of it, and it sprayed gas all over the room." From the way he described it, it sounded like it made a thick foam everywhere.

I also had another habit of wrapping .22 rifle shells in a piece of paper and throwing them in the trash can, hoping they would go off when the trash was burnt outside. I remember one day, Mr. Evans was making an announcement on the intercom, and said, "Please don't set fire to the trash cans before lunch time." I never did know whether or not it had anything to do with the shells that I had thrown in the trash.

I did an experiment at home. Someone had told me that if a bullet went off in a fire, it would shoot out just like it would if it was fired from a gun. I wanted to find out for sure if that was true. I took a .22 rifle shell and put it in a tin can full of pine straw. I set the tin can in a wheel barrow with the open end facing the sky. Then, I laid a piece of thin metal across the top of the wheel barrow. If the bullet shot out of it, it would make a hole somewhere. I set the straw on fire. In a little while, the bullet exploded. It did not make a hole. Another time, I built a fire and put a german lugar bullet in it. After it exploded, I found the bullet laying about a foot away from the fire.

After a couple of my schemes fell through, I found a medicine bottle and filled it with gasoline. Then I wrapped it in several layers of notebook paper with a .22 rifle bullet inside the layers of paper.

I was carrying it in my coat pocket. One day, during lunch period, I was in my room standing around. Jody Coltrane and some other people were there. Jody was fooling around, and bumped his hand into my coat pocket. "What's that in your pocket?," he playfully demanded.

"Nothing," I said. Then, halfway focusing on me, and listening to something someone was saying, he was distracted for a minute. When his back was turned, I slipped away quickly, took the package out of my pocket, and stuffed it behind the radiator that was toward the front of the room.

Out of the corner of his eye, he realized that I had been up to the front of the room. He asked again what I had in my pocket. I said, "Nothing." Then I really didn't have anything in my pocket.

Then, he said to me, "You hid something in your desk. Where's your desk?"

I replied, "Right there," indicating a desk that was located near the back of the room, not close to the front of the room.

He seemed to be a little puzzled. Then he didn't say anything else about it.

The package stayed behind the radiator for a few days. Then, one day I stuck the head of a match into the layers of paper and left the butt end of it sticking out like a wick.

One day, during lunch, I waited until everyone left the room. Richard Rose, a boy named Jeff, and myself were the only ones left in the room, and then when they left, I eased over to the radiator, lit the end of the match stem and went outside quickly. When I was at the north end of the building, I heard the bullet explode. The plan was for the bullet to bust the bottle and ignite the gasoline.

Just before recess was over, I went into the room. Right next to the radiator, where I set the fire, there was Aaron and two or three other boys grouped together talking. The air in the room looked, and smelled smoky. In an effort to make myself look innocent, I said to Aaron, "Do you'all smell smoke?" But they were engulfed in their conversation and didn't seem to pay me any mind.

Then in a few minutes, Mr. Todd came in. He looked around, and asked something like, "What's that smoking in here? Has somebody been burning papers in here?"

Aaron, and the boys that were talking to each other said, "Yeah, something's been smoking in here."

He walked over to the radiator and said threateningly, as he made eye contact with me, "Somebody did that while we were eating lunch. I'm gonna find out who done that and burn their rear end." (By this time, they had built a new lunch room. It was located at the south end of the back hall.)

I could sense by his tone that he didn't suspect me.

During class that afternoon, he was informing all the students, "Somebody's been burning papers in here, and I just about know who it is." He continued on lecturing the class about the incident. He said something to the effect, "If you were to burn this school building down, they'd send you to the electric chair."

As he was addressing the class, saying he just about knew who it was, it seemed like his eyes were blinking back and forth between Richard and Jeff. So I figured that he suspected them.

Jeff spoke up and said to him to the effect, "I heard something like a firecracker explode during recess."

He (Mr. Todd) replied, "I didn't hear that."

For the most part, I got along well with all my seventh grade teachers. But there was one that I really liked a level or two above any that I ever had. That was Mrs. Cooper. It's human nature, I suppose. She had a gentle personality that was very unusual. She was so nice to everyone. I have no remembrance of her ever scolding or being rough with anyone. This is not to say that she just let the students run over her. The thing is, I don't remember anyone ever misbehaving in her class. The way I felt about her, she was so nice we wouldn't want to act out of order. I would listen to anything she had to say about anything. It seemed like she had complete control of the class with her friendly personality. The irony is, that I sat in her class dreaming about burning down the school building.

One day, when we went to her class, she passed out the weekly readers and the headline read, "For $1000,000 would you give up your freedom?" There was a story about a man that gave up his freedom for $1000,000. The deal was, that he be locked up and sealed in a room for fifteen years. If at the end of that fifteen years, he had not been out of that room, the seal had not been broken, then he would be paid $1000,000.

She asked us if we thought we would give up our freedom for $1000,000.

I told her that there was no way that I would give up my freedom for $1000,000. She said to me, "So it's outta the question isn't it?"

Then, the man in the story changed his mind about giving up his freedom. A short time before the fifteen years was up, he told the man to keep his money. He was about forty years old, but looked much older. His hair was gray, and his body seemed to have aged faster than normal.

*H.H. Ezzard's daughter, *Jenny Jo asked me one day, "Do you know a teacher named, Mrs. Cooper?"

I answered something like, "Yeah, she's my english teacher."

She said, "I was talking to her the other day, and I asked her, `Do you know a boy named, Robert Massingill?' She said, `Yes, he just tries and tries to learn."

There was one occasion when we were discussing having various pets. We were talking about having different kinds of animals for pets, such as dogs, cats, birds or whatever. As we were leaving the class, I said to her, "I used to have a tame turtle."

She looked at me with a sparkle in her eye, and replied, "You had a tame turtle?" The story was that years before, I had found a dry land turtle in the woods. I kept it in a box with dirt and moss. It would eat out of my hand.

A lot of times, I would feed it worms. I would lay a worm out on the red formica table, and the turtle would run across the table like a football player about to tackle someone. It would rip up the worm and eat it.

Finally, I was advised by friends and family members that I should let it go. They advised me that it would eventually die if I kept it in captivity. So I took it to the edge of the woods on a sunny day. I set it down on the ground. I remember it sticking it's neck out as far as it could before the woods. It seemed to be confused about what to do. But it finally went on into the woods.

I suppose by the way I acted, none of the teachers would have suspected that I was trying to burn down the school building. Outwardly, I acted like an ordinary student. But only God Himself could see what was really going on. I never did stay back in the same grade. I always studied and learned what was necessary to pass.

But this year, I had trouble with history. Mrs. Collins would sternly admonish us to learn our history lesson. Many times, she would quiz us to see how much we had learned. One morning, she asked me a certain question. She would call on us at random. We never knew when she would call our name, so we had to pay attention.

Now, there was a certain occasion once, when Mrs. Hayes had said to us in her class, "If you're asked a question and you don't know the answer, at least make a stab at it."

I'm sure that most of the time, that's true. But this particular morning in Mrs. Collins's class, I'm not sure that was a good idea. Her question was, "Who turned traitor and fought with the

British?"

I had no idea who it was, but I did what Mrs. Hayes had said. I guessed and replied in a questionable tone, "George Washington?"

You could hear a pin drop. The class was deftly quiet. It was like everyone gasped for breath.

My answer didn't go over with her. She said some unplesant things to me, and expressed her astonishment that I said, "George Washington."

The year ended, and I was promoted to the eight grade.

The eight grade was in the high school building. The high school building was situated about a quarter of a mile or less behind the elementary school.

Unlike the elementary building, it had only one hall. But it had two separate buildings. It had one building on the south side of the main building (hereafter referred to as the secondary building). The cafeteria was on the north end of the main building. The gymnasium was a separate building on the north side of the main building.

On the north wall of the secondary building was the boys bathroom window. If you were not a tall person, as I was not, you might have a problem with this bathroom. The door handle on the inside of the door was gone. If you were inside by yourself, you couldn't get out unless you were tall enough to reach the top of the door. There was a crack wide enough to pry open the door with your fingers. But if you were no taller that I was, (a little over five feet) there was only one thing left; climb out the window. Many times, this was the way I exited the bathroom.

Halfway up the main building, if you are going north, the next boys bathroom is on the left wing (hereafter referred to as the lower left wing) just before the exit. At the north end of the hall, there is the next left wing, (hereafter referred to as the north left wing) and again there is a boys bathroom just before the exit. Next to the wing, at the end of the hall is the cafeteria.

Now, here was the problem; the high school was a newer building than the elementary school. It seemed to have been built with so much concrete and steel, that I decided that it was not going to burn.

Although I figured the building wouldn't burn, I was bound and determined to do all the damage to it that I could. Also, there was something else that lay ahead that would raise the stakes, and make the game even more dangerous.

DIAGRAM 3
HIGH SCHOOL LAYOUT

```
BAND ROOM          WOOD WORKING SHOP
I-----------------------------------I
I                  I                 I
I                  I                 I
I                  I                 I
I                  I                 I
I                  I                 I
I                  I                 I
I-----------------------------------I


                   LOWER LEFT                      NORTH
                     WING                        LEFT WING

I-------------------------III-----------------------------------III------I
I                                                             I  L   I
I   E                     HIGH SCHOOL                         I  U   I
I S N                                                         I  N   I
I O T                   MAIN BUILDING                         I  C   I
- U R                                                         I  H   I
I T A                                                         I  R   I
I H N                                                         I  O   I
I   C                                                         I  O   I
I   E                                          FRONT          I  M   I
I-----------------------------------------------III--------------------I
                                              ENTRANCE
```

CHAPTER SIX
A TIME OF WAR

Do you remember the 1960's series, ,The Fugitive ? Dr. Richard Kimble was falsely convicted and sentenced to the electric chair for killing his wife. The Police Lieutenant was obsessed with his capture. Dr. Kimble saw the real killer, a man with one arm leaving the crime scene. He was on the run, cross-country searching for the one armed man. At the same time, he was running from the Police to save his own life.

I was in the sixth grade when it first came on. Mama worked second shift at the cotton mill and Daddy had to leave between 10:30 and 11:00 to pick her up. ,The Fugitive came on at 10:00 and went off at 11:00. Daddy would watch it until he had to leave to go get Mama. He would ask me the next day how it ended. I always got a strange thrill out of telling him, "He got away."

I was fascinated with the program. Up until now, I was used to seeing the person on the outside of the law always get caught. There were westerns, detective pictures, and all sorts of programs. But not like this. It had a different spin.

Although it was fiction, it was loosely based on the true story of Sam Sheperd, who was accused of killing his wife. He was convicted of murder in the second degree, and sent to prison. Later, he won a new trial and was acquitted because of new evidence.

By the time I had reached junior high, I was hooked on the program. In my fantasy, I compared myself to Richard Kimble. He was innocent, running from the law. I considered myself a victim of the school system. As Richard Kimble was a fugitive from the law, I considered myself a fugitive from the school system, trying to destroy it without getting caught.

I did not believe in stealing. I very rarely ever stole anything. For instance, if I saw someone's watch, pocket knife, lunch money, or any other valuables sitting on their desk, I wouldn't think of stealing it, even if I knew for sure I could get away with it.

One day during the seventh grade, myself and another boy were in the classroom by ourselves. He was going through people's coat pockets to see if there was anything in them. I asked him, "You mean that if there was any money in those pockets, you'd steal it?"

"Yeah, I would," he replied. As I remember the incident, his answer surprised me.

But school property was different. I had declared war on the school. I didn't consider it stealing, I considered it getting even.

I remember once when I was in the seventh grade, I stole new literature books from my english class. There was a blonde headed boy named Steven Cole, that was in the same grade as Stanley North. (Although Stanley was a year older than I was, he was about three grades behind me.) That year, they were in the same room. One day, as I was sitting next to Steven on the school bus, I gave him a literature book and told him to take it home. I explained to him how the school system allegedly took advantage of us, and that it wasn't stealing. He looked dumbfounded at the time, and I never knew what he did with the book.

School. It was a cuss word. School messed up my life. I thought my life would be perfect if it hadn't been for school.

The way I had things figured out reminds me of a story I heard once on a Christian radio station. The name of the program was ,Unshackled.

The young boy was a drug dealer. He sold cocaine and whatever else was available illegally. Through a process of events, he got introduced to The Bible and The Gospel. He read the scripture in Proverbs, Chapter Sixteen, Verse Eleven, that says, "A just weight and balance are The Lord's; all the weights of the bag are His work." So, whenever he sold a certain amount of cocaine, or whatever he was selling, he would weigh it on a small scale to make sure it was right.

He read in the twentieth chapter of Exodus about keeping the sabbath day. Then, he would not sell drugs on Sunday. When someone came to his house on Sunday, to buy some drugs, he wouldn't sell them any. He said he would explain to them that The Bible says not to work on the sabbath. He said he stayed this way until through a series of events, God really delivered him from all of it.

He had things figured out about like I did.

During my seventh year, I became acquainted with a certain boy about my size, named, Shane Sinclair who had black hair that was neatly combed stright back from his forehead. He was in Mrs. Cooper's home room. One sunny day during recess, he and I were playfully fist fighting on the sidewalk behind the back hall. As we were slugging at each other, several boys gathered around us, thinking that we were really fighting. By accident, I hit him in the nose. As blood ran from his nose, a certain boy with brown hair, who was a little taller than me, named Richie, that I knew since the fifth grade, hollered, "Hit'im Robert."

Then, to everyone's amazement, we both grinned and walked away. From that point on, we became good friends.

This year however, we were in the same room. During the seventh grade, I had told him nothing about my plan to burn down the school. But this year, I shared everything with him.

Leon Garrett and I were still friends, but we didn't hang around each other as much. If he had been a detective, he would have caught me at my foul play. I never was really sure why, but it seemed that he had me figured out. One thing it may have been was, that on one occasion, I had drawn a picture of a dog on the outside door of the lower left wing with a black marker.

He had seen some of my lousy drawing on paper a year before. He could tell that it matched. He asked me, "Ain't that some of your drawing like you did last year?"

I denied it, saying "No, it ain't." So maybe he tied it in with everything else.

My homeroom teacher's name was Mrs. Battles, a young lady about my height who had lengthy brown hair. Unlike the seventh grade, our homeroom teacher did not teach any of our classes. So the only time we were in her room was for a short time, about ten or fifteen minutes early in the morning. I suppose she was probably glad of it because we aggravted her something awful, just to hear her yell at us. For instance, we would talk and act silly while she was trying to make announcements and so forth.

There was a registration fee of $1.25 that the school charged everybody in the beginning of each year. I don't remember exactly when it started, but that was one of those things that a lot of people rebelled against, myself included. We accused the school officials, or the principal of concocting this thing just so they could put it in their pocket. The princuipal, Mr. Monahan, a tall elderly man with graying hair would come around to the classes sometimes and ask, "Who all owes the office a dollar and a quarter?"

On different occasions, Mrs. Battles would admonish the class to pay the registration fee. A tall, heavy set boy named, Ralph French, who reminded me of the actor, Slim Pickens sat behind me and would mumble rebelliously, "I don't owe you no dollar and a quarter."

One morning when she was addressing the class about this, she said to the effect, "Everyone needs to pay their regestration fee." Then, she glared over at Ralph, and said, "Don't sit over there and say, I don't owe you no dollar and a quarter."

One morning, the assistant principal, Mr. Cline, a mediun built man with short dark hair, probably in his thirties, made an announcement that he wanted to see the following people in room two. Then, he proceeded to call names. He called many names, including my own as he went on. No one seemed to have any idea why we were called into this room. As we were all seated in whichever desk we chose, waiting for him to come in, everyone was talking and whispering to each other. There was a heavy set boy in a higher grade than I was who sat across the aisle from me. I asked him, "Do you know why we're called in here?"

He answered, "I donno."

I replied, "I think I know."

He asked, "What?"

I answered, "I think it's because we haven't paid our regestration fee." I asked him to the effect, whether or not he had paid his, and he said that he had not.

Then, he started asking everyone who was sitting close to him, "Have you paid your regestration fee?" They all said that they had not.

Sure enough, when Mr. Cline came into the room, he informed us that this was the reason we were called in there. He went down the row and asked each person when they were going to pay it. Most of the people said they would pay it as soon as they could, or put up some excuse about it. I remember a certain boy named Jason Clark that I had known since the third grade, that was there. He asked him when he was going to pay his, and he answered defiantly, "I ain't gonna pay it." He made no further comment to him.

Somewhere in the course of this, he called my name. I said to him, "I'll pay it when I get it."

He worked out a deal with some of us. He let some of us work it out sweeping floors. So, this is the way I worked mine out. But I suppose that in the long run, the school came up short considering all the damage I did.

Mr. Madison, a tall, slim, sandy headed man who had his hair cut short was our math teacher in first period. He also was our physical education coach in second period (hereafter referred to as P.E.) with the assistance of another coach named, Mr. Graves, who looked like Captain Binghamton on ,McHale's Navy . He wore black rimmed glasses like him. He was the same height, with the same color of hair, and his wife, who had reddish brown hair, and filled in as a substitute teacher sometimes, said, "He hollers like'im."

As I was sitting next to him on the bleachers in the gym during an event, I asked him, "You know who you look like?"

He asked, "Who?"

I replied, "Captain Binghamton on ,McHale's Navy ."

He replied smoothly as he gazed out over the gym floor, "I wish I had his money."

I really liked both of these teachers, Mr. Madison and Mr. Graves. I also liked Mrs. Graves, when she filled in as a substitute teacher.

Now, the first half of the year, instead of having P.E., we had health class. Mr. Graves was the teacher. One morning, he came into the classroom and sat down in his desk. Then he proclaimed to us in a sharp tone, "I feel terrible. If I don't start felling better pretty soon, I'm gonna start gettin' mean."

Later, I thought to myself, "He must've started felling better, he never did get mean."

Up until now, I had always plotted to burn down the elementary building with gasoline or some other flammable liquid. The same plot continued in the high school building, but in my third period class, which was science, I was about to get introduced to something more dangerous. Our teacher, Mr. Alexander, used chemicals to do experiments in his science and chemistry classes. Dangerous chemicals. Full strength sulfuric acid. Nitric acid. Hydrochloric acid. Strangely enough, he had many other acids and oxides sitting openly on shelves in the classroom. The walls were lined with shelves and acid proof sinks.

Once when we went into his classroom, he had a small whiskey still set up on a table running white lightening.

Some of the boys were laughing about it and I heard Ralph French say, "Alexander's running off moonshine."

Since the building wouldn't burn, I devised a plot to smuggle some acid out of the science room while no one was looking. I was planning to put acid on the building and destroy anything I could. But there was a problem. What I did not know was, that the acid had to be stored in acid proof containers. One day, I filled up a vitamin pill bottle with sulfuric acid, and took it home to experiment. I wanted to find out what it would destroy and what it wouldn't. But the next thing I knew, it burned the pocket liners out of my coat. It would soak through the ordinary glass bottle. I wore a black furry coat and had a lot of extra space in it after the linings were gone.

One morning, I slipped to the back of the room while no one was noticing, and filled up a pill bottle with nitric acid. I put it in my paints pocket and went to my seat. About a half a minute later, I ran my hand in my pocket and felt the acid soaking out of the bottle. I quickly eased to the back and poured it down the sink. Sulfuric was the only acid I could smuggle out of the room. There were times when the students did experiments with various acids. They submerged a penny in sulfuric acid and it turned as silver as a dime.

In P.E. class, we were required to take exercises of different kinds. They told us to bring a pair of shorts to dress out in. A lot of the boys, including myself would try to get out of it. As ironic as it sounds, anything we were required to do, we would rebell against. On some days, they wouldn't make us dress out. I would volunteer to sweep the floor in an attempt to get out of it. Sometimes it would work and sometimes it wouldn't. One morning, I walked up to Mr. Graves and asked, "Do you want me to sweep the floor?"

He responded sharply, "No, I want you to get dressed out for P.E."

As soon as his back was turned, I slipped away and hid behind the stage. The stage was facing the gym floor, but it had a space behind it about eighteen inches wide. I hid in the darkness about halfway in the middle. Then I heard his sharp voice calling the row. I heard him call my name. He called out, "Robert Massingill; is he here?"

After I heard him call my name, I sneaked out from behind the stage, and went outside behind the building. When I got out there, there were three or four more boys hiding out there. They were standing out there with their breeches legs rolled up to their knees. In retrospect, they looked very comical standing out there the way they were. I guess they had them rolled up in case they got caught, they would be ready to do exercises.

During that entire year, I never did dress out for P.E. The closest I ever came to dressing out, was on one particular morning, when I brought a pair of shorts. I had already put them on when a certain small framed, boy with curly blonde hair that I was acquainted with, named, Josh Watson said to me, "You'd better get your clothes back on."

"How come?" I asked.

He said, "We're not dressing out today."

Apparently, Mr. Madison and Mr. Graves both saw something in me that they liked. I was always willing and ready to help clean things up, and things of this nature. And also, Shane was in on it. The two of us at face value stood out above the others. We ran together and most of the time when someone saw one of us, they saw the other.

Every chance I got, I would break coke deposit bottles. In the east area in front of the gym, there was a picnic shed. The area was shaded with oak trees. One day, I was out in front of it and noticed a bunch of coke bottles scattered all around in the grass. No one was looking, so I broke all of them.

The next day, we were out there, and a certain boy said to Mr. Graves, "Mr. Graves, somebody broke ever one of these coke bottles."

We all got together and cleaned up the piles of broken glass. I was right in the middle of cleaning it up. I had my hands full of broken glass and I remember Mr. Graves saying to me, "Be careful, that'll cut the dickance out of you."

During the previous summer, I caught something in the woods that started out like poison oak. It made sores, that became scabs. I don't know what it was, but it finally set up blood poison in my left leg. One Saturday, my leg was throbbing like a toothache. Mama and Daddy took me to the emergency room. I was taken in and our family doctor was called. Our doctor's assistant arrived and did his diagnoses. Unknown to me, he called Mama and Daddy out in the hall, and said to them to the effect, "His leg's full of blood poison. It's about to turn into gangrene. If it turns into gangrene, it'll spread through his body, and he'll die. We're gonna have to amputate his leg at the knee."

The doctor told them that the blood poison had been set off by a lick of some kind. However, unknown to the doctor, my younger brother, Michael (we called him Mike), and I had had a scuffle a few days earlier. During the course of it, I was accidently hit on top of one of the sores with a broken gun stock. The way I understood it, it was a good thing that I got hit on the leg. Otherwise, the blood poison would have been more deadly.

Mama and Daddy didn't know what to do. They were trying to figure out what to do when *Dr. Whitfield, an elderly doctor overheard the conversation. He happened to be at the hospital to check on a patient. He interfered and wanted to look at my leg. I didn't know what was going on when he came in. He didn't say much. In retrospect, he reminded me a little bit of Doc Adams on ,Gunsmoke. He tore the seams of my blue jeans up my leg. He took a needle, and put deadening fluid in my leg to kill the feeling.

I was laying there looking up at the ceiling, day dreaming. Then I decided to raise up and see what was going on. I was surprised at what I saw. I saw a large hole in my leg that went to the bone. I was fascinated because I couldn't feel it.

But after I got to looking at it, it seemed like it was starting to hurt. I said to one of the nurses, "It's starting to hurt a little now."

Then, she explained something like, "That's because you're looking at it. It's in your mind. As long as you don't look at it, it won't hurt."

Through the process of this operation, he drained out all of the blood poison. So they didn't have to take my leg off.

The first night that I was in the hospital, I got up to go to the bathroom. They didn't tell me not to get out of the bed (or at least they didn't make it clear to me). As I was climbing back into the bed, I felt faint like, and then fell over into the bed.

The next morning, I awoke to find the nurses changing the bandages on my leg. A certain nurse with reddish brown hair said to me sternly, "You outta be spanked." She went on to say something like, "You're not supposed to get up on that leg." Apparently, when I got up, my leg was pouring blood into the bandages. Then, I understood why I was feeling faint when I climbed back into the bed.

Later that day, she came by the room, and again she said to me firmly, "Don't you get up no more."

One day, when I was in a deep sleep, I was awakened by the man who was in the room with me. He had been hospitilazed with a medical problem similar to mine. He was a slim elderly man with thinning gray hair. I opened my eyes and as he propped himself on one arm, he was trying to hand me the phone receiver with his other hand. Daddy was on the other end of the line. But I was under such heavy medication, that my mind wasn't working right. I thought that he was trying to get me to hold the receiver instead of laying it on the hook. In my mind, the receiver was supposed to be hung on top of the tele- phone. I took it from his hand, and then, hung it up. Afterwards, I remembered the incident, but at the time, I didn't know what I was doing.

I stayed in the hospital for a week. When I got out of the

hospital, I could walk, but I couldn't run at all. After a while, my strength came back and I could run as always.

But what surprised me, was how nice the other boys at school treated me. I got a letter from the homeroom class while I was in the hospital. They were saying nice things to me wishing me to get well.

One person who surprised me was Jody Coltrane. Although he and I were not enemies, we really were not considered friends. There were times before this that we got along well, and then there were times that we did not. One day, during the afternoon recess, as he and I were sitting in a certain classroom, he was talking to me very nice, and replied, "I heard they were gonna cut both of your legs off."

One day, right after these things, I was standing behind the gym. Some of the other boys were there also. Inspite of everything that happened, I was feeling anger toward the school. They all were standing with their backs turned. There were some windows high up at the top of the gym, and while they weren't looking, I was going to try to throw a rock and break a window. When I threw the rock, it hit the back of the gym and bounced off. One of the boys turned around and asked me softly, "Did you throw a rock?"

I don't remember what I said to him, but I put up some excuse and said, "Yeah, I was throwing at the back of the gym."

Through my home research, I discovered that sulfuric acid would destroy almost any kind of cloth or paper I put it on. I tried it on concrete. As far as I could tell, it did not do anything to concrete. I tried it on wood, but it did nothing to wood. I tested it to see if it was flammable, but it was not.

I studied in chemistry books about the different kinds of acids. According to what information I gathered, nitric acid would attack steel. The book also said it would turn the skin a deep yellow. The question in my mind was, what else would it do after it turned the skin yellow?

I figured out how to carry sulfuric acid. A small brown nose drop bottle would fit snuggly, and stand upright inside a regular sized mustard jar. I carried a mustard jar inside my coat with a bottle of acid in it.

Many times, I poured a little on a roll of toilet paper in the bathrooms. Also, on paper bulletins that were on the walls of classrooms, or wherever I could do some damage.

On one occasion, I put some acid on a paper product on a bulleton board at the back of a certain classroom. Leon Garrett turned around in his seat and saw me holding a small brown bottle. "What's that? "he asked.

I replied, "Nose drops." That time, he bought my little story.

I also researched on how to make nitroglycerin. I learned that strongly mixed nitrosulfuric acid mixed with glycerin would produce nitroglycerin. Nitrosulfuric was nothing more than nitric and sulfuric mixed together. I was also aware of how dangerous it was. I had planned not to be close to the mixture when it was mixed. I was planning to put each of the acids in separate test tubes, and the glycerin in another test tube. Then set the test tubes inside a large container. I planned to have a string tied to the lower part of each test tube, a string tied to the large container, and be a long way off. Then, I planned to pull the strings to mix the chemicals together. Then, I planned to pull the large container off a high place to make it explode. But there was a major problem. I couldn't find any glycerin. I didn't even know what it was. The chemistry book said it was a liquid with a sweet taste like syrup.

I also studied up on the subject of mixing certain acids together. I learned that mixing nitric and hydrochloric acids together would produce an acid that was suppose to destroy anything. The book said it would dissolve gold.

Our fourth period class was study hall. The room was in the secondary building. During that class, we could study anything we wanted. There was just certain basic rules we had to follow. The teacher in charge was a young, dark haired lady, named, Mrs. Lansing. She looked to be in her twenties.

For some reason, she had a personality that caused a lot of the boys to want to aggravate her just to hear her gripe at them. She hardly ever smiled or laughed. She always had a look of seriousness on her face. Not that she was mean or anything, actually, she was easy to get along with. She was just all business.

The only time I recall her laughing, was on a certain occasion, when a certain boy kept complaining that he was hungry. (We went to lunch during fourth period, so I suppose it was close to lunch time.) She tried to get him to be patient. She said to him, "Why don't you get your book and study it?"

Apparently, he didn't have it with him, so she let him leave the room long enough to go get it. When he returned to the room, he had only the front and back covers to it. He said to her, "This is all that's left of it."

The entire class roared with laughter, and for once, I saw her laugh. I heard someone say, "You're not that hungry are you?"

To me, this was an unusual class. People from every grade were there. I liked it because we had a certain amount of freedom that we didn't have in any of our other classes.

One day, she (Mrs. Lansing) asked how many of us were not eating lunch. If we didn't eat, we stayed in the room. I said to her, "I'm not eating today, but I usually do eat."

Making eye contact with me in her business like manner, she questioned me, "You usually do eat?"

I said, "Yeah."

On a certain rainy day, Shane and I were on our way back from the lunchroom. But we stopped at the south end of the main building. We were standing outside under the drip of the building causally watching the raindrops fall from the roof. Then I looked down the landscape and spied her (Mrs. Lansing) standing with her hands on the sides of her hips, staring at us. Then, in a way what seemed comical to us, she proclaimed, "Get in here!"

I remember on one occasion, she left the room for a few minutes. While she was gone, several of the boys who were in a higher grade than I was, were talking and carrying on. One of them spied out the door and saw her coming down the sidewalk from the main building. He said to the others, "Here she comes!"

When she walked into the room, they all looked innocent. Then she informed them that she heard them before she got there. She replied, "I heard, `Here she comes."

Many times, when I got the chance, I would throw entire rolls of toilet paper into the commodes. One day, when I was on one of my usual rampages, I left the study hall room during lunch period (the others had already gone to lunch a little bit ahead of me) with the intention of destroying every roll I could. I went into the bathroom which was right down the hall from the study hall, and threw in all the rolls that I saw. Then, I climbed out the window, and entered the south end of the main building. Midway up the hall, I stopped by the lower left wing and did the same thing. I exited it and headed up the hall with the intention of raiding the one at the north left wing.

I subconsciously noticed when I came out the door of the bathroom, that I met a tall, heavy set teacher with dark hair, named, Mr. Henderson, whose room was right down the hall from our study hall. He looked like his mouth was halfway opened as if he was going to say something. As I started up the hall, I met Mrs. Lansing coming back from the lunchroom. She asked me, "Where're you going?"

I replied, "To the lunchroom."

"Why didn't you leave when the others did?" she inquired.

I replied, "I got caught in the crowds in the hallway."

Then, Mr. Henderson walked up and said, "You left after the hall was completely clear. You went into the bathroom down there, then, climbed out the window. Then, you went into this bathroom down here, and I followed you all the way."

I replied, "The door don't have a handle, and I can't reach

the top of it. I went into this bathroom down here to wash my hands from climbing out the window down there."

"Okay," he said. "But don't let it happen again."

So then, I went on to the lunchroom to make it look good. When I got to the lunchroom, I didn't have any money to eat because I had squandered my lunch money. I told Mrs. Tatum, a short, middle aged lady with graying hair, that I didn't have any money, but I would pay her the next day. So, they let me eat on credit and I paid them the next day.

There was a teacher named, Mr. Ralston, a medium built man with dark thinning hair who taught my sixth period english class. He also drove the bus that I rode. Every afternoon, he left a little earily and trusted our class to behave on our own. Also, he filled in for Mrs. Lansing in our fourth period study hall. As far as I remember, he took that class over after so long.

There was also a teacher named Mrs. Cannon who taught my fifth period, Georgia History class for the first part of the year. She was about my height, medium built and dark headed. The kids gave her a nickname that she didn't know about. It wasn't anything bad, she had a reputation for being a detective. If there had been some mischief done, she was good at finding out who did it. Her nickname was double 0 seven.

Most of the time, Mr. Madison and Mr. Graves called us by our last names. It was an unusual thing if he called us by our first names.

A lot of times, they would send different ones of us out to pick up paper off the ground. I remember once, when Mr. Madison sent Shane and I out to pick up paper in a certain area. We worked for a long time bagging bags of paper off the ground. Later, he said to me, "You and Sinclair did a good job."

One day, Shane, myself, and Josh Watson were sent out to pick up paper behind the main building. Shane said to us jokingly, "Boys, I'm gonna go right around here. When I get back, I expect all this paper to be... up."

Josh chuckled at him, saying to the effect, "Oh no, you

don't! You're gonna help us pick up this paper."

There was a boy named Scott Lanier that was in our class. He was about my size with brown hair. Shane and I associated with him, but like all the others, he didn't know about the destruction we were plotting against the school. One morning, I heard some of the boys talking about an incident that just occurred. They said, "Scott Lanier shattered the basketball backboard with a marble." Now, the backboards on the basketball goals were made of fiberglass. Not realizing what he was doing, he threw the marble against the backboard and shattered it."

As far as I know, he was not punished for this little accident. They understood that he just didn't realize how easy it would be for a marble to break it.

Mr. Graves gathered all of us in the gym and gave the class a strong lecture about taking care of things, tearing things up and so forth. It was almost like he was rebuking the whole class for the backboard being shattered. During his lecture, Mr. Madison and some helpers were knocking out the pieces of shattered fiberglass onto a mat in the floor. I remember Mr. Madison climbing up on a ladder behind the backboard and kicking it out with his foot. During the course of it, I remember him saying something like, "Now, this youngster didn't mean to do this." Then, he went on to say to the effect, "If you don't think it's a big job keeping things cleaned up, ask Massingill and Sinclair."

I was constantly smuggling acid, various kinds of household chemicals, and other objects in the linings of my coat, looking for a chance to do some kind of damage. Some of the objects consisted of test tubes, medicine droppers, and things I stole from the science room. One certain object I carried was a medium sized screwdriver. In every classroom, there were radiators covered with sheet metal held together with screws. Every chance I got, I would take a screw out of the radiator. I took apart anything I could. Many times, I would take the nuts and bolts out of the bleachers in the gym, or the bleachers on the football field.

One afternoon, during the fifteen minute recess, Shane and I were fooling around in the classroom, taking screws out of the radiator. The radiator was right in front of the windows. As I held the screwdriver in front of the window, turning a screw, Shane said to me, "Watch out, somebody'll see you."

We took out one screw too many. There were no more screws left in the radiator and the big piece of sheet metal was about to slide off in the floor. Shane took a piece of plastic and stuck it in one of the screw holes to temporarily hold it on.

A certain girl who was in the room saw that we were having trouble getting it to stay on. She asked us, "What'd you'all do to it?"

I replied, "We didn't do nothing to it."

Then, recess being over, everyone came into the room and took their seats. Mr. Ralston took his seat. Just as everything got quiet and in order, the piece of plastic let go. Then, the big piece of sheet metal slammed onto the green tile floor, and immediately had everyone's attention. Mr. Ralston sat behind his desk, asking, "Who done it?,... Who done it?," over and over.

Shane and I were the top suspects. A girl named Angie said to Shane, "You did it."

I said, "No, he didn't do it."

"You both did it," she responded.

After a minute or so, Shane said to me, "Robert, you'd better get rid of that screwdriver."

I quietly scolded at him, "Shut up!"

Mr. Ralston called Mr. Monahan down to our room to help solve this problem. He stood in front of it and said, "Well, now that it's down, let's get all of that trash out from behind it."

Some of the boys in the class got a trash can and cleaned the filth and trash off the inner parts that were exposed. Mr. Monahan said something to Shane to imply that he was the one who did it.

Shane said, "I didn't do it."

He responded, "Yeah, you did."

Everybody, including Mr. Ralston and Mr. Monahan figured that either Shane, myself, or both of us took the screws out of it. But the whole thing finally died down.

One day, we were fooling around in one of our classrooms and I was putting sulfuric acid on something in the room. A minute or two later, I sat down in my seat, and Shane sat down in the seat in front of mine. Then, he glanced at the forearm of my coat sleeve and exclaimed to me quietly, "Looka there!" I looked down at my coat sleeve and saw what looked like a small volcano. I had accidently squirted acid on my coat sleeve with a medicine dropper.

One morning, when we were in science class, we were seated next to a certain area of the room, where there was a bottle of nitric acid setting on the shelf. Shane whispered to me, "I think I'll take some of that acid down to Lansing's room." He had a Dristan bottle he was going to put it in.

I whispered to him saying to the effect, "You can't carry nitric acid in a pill bottle. It'll soak through it as soon as you put it in there."

But he insisted on it anyway. I tried and tried to get him not to do it. We whispered back and forth debating the issue. I lost the argument. Just before class changed, he poured some acid in the bottom of the bottle. Then, the bell rang. The hallway was full of students going to their next class. Being that our science room was in the north section of the main building, we had to pass by the bathroom on the way to our study hall class.

On the way down the hall, he ran his hand into his pocket. He felt the acid soaking out into his pocket. We went into the bathroom and wrapped it in many layers of toilet paper. As we walked down the hallway, he held it in his hand, as the toilet paper dissolved away. Steam was rising off it as if it was boiling water. Then, his fingers turned deep yellow like the chemistry book said. But what scared me was, that I didn't know what else it would do. The book just said it would turn the skin a deep yellow. I thought maybe that meant the color it would turn before it burned your fingers off. I had also studied about the effects of poisoning by this particular acid. The book described many horrifying symptoms that would happen before death occurred.

As we discovered through experience, nitric acid will not hurt your fingers. His fingers turned yellow, and that's all it did. In retrospect, I suppose it's a good thing he didn't have any cut places on his hands.

I was afraid we were going to get caught with the acid. When we got to the study hall, I sat on the opposite side of the room from him.

Mr. Alexander, an elderly man who was heavy set with thinning hair was having health problems. Mrs. Graves was filling in as a substitute in his place. But we were not in the usual science room. We were just up the hall from the lower left wing.

Sad to say, the students in our class gave him a hard time. It may have contributed to his health problems. As far as I understood it, he had heart trouble. He had several fights with some of the students. One day, he had the heat on, and a certain boy named Alfred was sitting next to the window. Alfred had opened the window because to him, it was hot. Suddenly, Mr. Alexander rushed over and angrily closed the window, saying something to the effect, "I try to keep it warn in here, and you let all the heat out!"

Then Alfred retorted, "Well, it's hot over here beside this blame radiator!"

Now, at the top of the wall next to the hallway, there were some big windows. When he and Alfred had their little spat, he noticed that all three of them were opened. He picked up a long rod that was used to open and close them, and started closing them. As he was closing the last one, the rod slipped and broke the glass. A piece of glass fell from the window and clattered behind the shelves that lined the wall.

After class was over, everyone was laughing at him behind his back, for breaking the window.

One day, I took a plastic shampoo tube and filled it with gasoline. I smuggled it to school in my coat. That morning, while I was in Mrs. Graves's room, the gas tube sprung a leak. I took it out of my coat pocket and put it in the bottom of the desk I was sitting in.

Shane asked me, "Do you have a cap on it?"

I said, "Yeah."

He looked at it and replied, "You've got a stick in it."

I said, "I know, but that's not where it's leaking. It's leaking out the bottom."

Mrs. Graves was standing in the front of the class and asked us, "What do they heat this building with?"

There was a two inch pipe that ran under the radiator from room to room, that carried whatever type of heat it carried. As far as I can remember, they had a furnace. I don't remember what anybody said, but she went on to say, "I smell gasoline. Does anyone in here have any gasoline on you?"

We all denied having any on us. Everyone was saying, "No, I don't."

When class changed, I left the leaking tube in the desk I was sitting in, and went on to fourth period. Some of the gasoline leaked into my clothes, and there were rumors of gasoline vapors everywhere. As I sat next to the window in the sun, I adjusted myself to where the rays would shine directly on my wet clothes. Before long, my clothes had dried out.

I remember someone asking Mr. Ralston something like, "Do you think we're all gonna get blowed up by those gas fumes?" As far as I remember, he gave no answer. Just by reading his facial expression, he seemed to be mystified as to where the fumes were coming from."

Sometime afterward, Shane said to me, "I took the desk that you was sitting in, and switched it with another one so they won't know who put the gasoline in it."

During study hall, they always gave out passes to go to the library to the ones who were going. For instance, if we were going to do some research on a certain assignment, we could get a pass to go to the library.

Oftentimes, we went to the library. But a lot of times we just went up there to play around and kill time.

One day, a tall, dark headed young man with neatly trimmed short hair who was a library aid came over and asked me as I was sitting at the end of a shellacked table, "What'd you come up here for?" He asked me this because he knew I was just goofing off.

I came up with an excuse and answered, "I was looking for information about the Civil War."

Sometime before this, Mr. Ralston had been teaching us about the Civil War in Georgia History class. We had class discussion about the different events. I remember us talking about General Sherman and how he came through Georgia, leaving a path of destruction. I remember a certain boy named Curt Green (the same boy who threathened to call the Police on Mrs. Parker in the second grade, years before), who spoke up and said, "They came right by my house."

"Well, you're not gonna find it in there," he replied, indicating the colorful comic strips I was reading.

I said something like, "I know, I was just looking at these." So, to make things look good, I looked up some information about the Civil War.

I developed a habit of stealing the labels off the shelves. For instance, if a certain section was about United States History, that is what the label would read. Or I would snatch the envelope out of the back of the library books. Anything I could get my hands on, I would destroy.

I didn't intend to get too many at one time. They would figure out who was doing it. But the next thing I knew, Shane would come to me with a whole handful, and then, hand them to me. I tried to get him not to swipe so many. But that didn't work, and we over played our hand.

One day, as I started to leave the library, I had my back pushed against the swinging doors, and had them halfway opened as I was waiting for Shane. Then, one of the aids motioned for me to come back in. Shane was standing there where he was. He said, "Mrs. Blackwell (the head librarian) wants to see you."

She came out to where we were, glared at us and asked demandingly, "Where're my labels?"

We replied, "We ain't got no labels."

She retorted, "You've been going around from shelf to shelf taking my labels. You've been taking the brackets out from under the shelves. You think I don't know what's going on, but I know what you've been doing!"

"But we didn't," I said.

She retorted something like, "Don't tell me `No'! I don't take `No,' when it's a story!"

She barred us from the library. She said to us, "Don't come back in here until I say you can."

As we entered the study hall room, Mr. Ralston was standing behind the lectern, and asked us, "What've you'all been doing? Have you been into any trouble?"

We told him that we had not. Then, he said, "Let's go." As we were walking up the sidewalk toward the main building, he said to us, "We're gonna find out what you've got in those pockets."

We were headed toward the janitor's room which was north of the boys bathroom on the lower left wing, but south of the principal's office. The principal's office was on the right wing at the front entrance. The library was across the wing from the office.

On the way there, Shane whispered to me, "Do you have anything?"

I answered, "No."

Now, everyday I had been carrying sulfuric acid, and all the other things I carried. But the strangest thing had happened. That morning before I left for school, I clean forgot and left all the stuff at home. The only thing I had in my pocket was a medicine dropper that I had swiped from the science room, and a pair of dice.

We went into the janitor's room and he searched Shane's pockets first. Then, he said to me, "Unzip you're coat, Robert."

I slipped the medicine dropper up my coat sleeve. (Each sleeve had elastic that fitted snuggly around my wrists.) He felt all in my pockets and the only thing he found was the dice. He said to me, "You can keep the dice. I'm lookin' for library labels."

We had already disposed of the library labels, so he didn't find anything on us.

They also sent us to the principal's office. We told Mr. Monahan that we didn't do it. He said to us something like, "Oh, boys, you know how it is; you slide across a shelf here, and the labels disappear. Then you slide across a shelf over there and they disappear."

Mrs. Cannon came to the office and questioned us. As before, we denied all of it. She asked us, "You're not lying are you?"

We answered, "No."

This incident occurred on a Monday. That following Friday, I brought a shampoo tube to school filled with kerosene. I had it wrapped in several layers of notebook paper.

On this particular day, we were in Mrs. graves's science room above the lower left wing. I never knew why, and at the time, I didn't care, but she (Mrs. Graves) was lax on keeping everybody in their seats. Ordinarily, any school teacher required everybody to stay in their seats during class, and not to be up running around. She wasn't very strict about this. A person could actually leave the room to go to the bathroom, or the water fountain, and nothing would be said. (The water fountain was between our class and the bathroom.)

We were in class discussion, and no one was paying any attention to who was going out of the room and who wasn't.

At the beginning of third period, I had been in the bathroom looking for a chance to set something on fire. A certain blonde headed boy who was a little taller than I was, named Daniel Packard was just leaving the bathroom when I entered. Then, no one else was in there. As I was leaving, I poured some kind of a flammable liquid on the light switch that was right beside the door and set it on fire. (Now, oftentimes, I would take the light switch cover off and destroy it. There's no telling how many times I did this.) It didn't do anything but burn the liquid off the light switch cover, as I figured that that's all it would do.

As I exited the bathroom, Mr. Graves was sitting behind his desk facing his class that was across the hall. In plain view, he could see me coming out of the bathroom. But he could not see that I had set fire to the light switch.

Shane and I were seated in the aisle next to the door of the classroom, toward the front. Sometime during the mid part of third period, I slipped out of the room and walked into the bathroom. Mr. Graves's door was now closed so he could keep out the sounds from the hall. That way, he couldn't see out. No one was around and everything was quiet. I took the tube of kerosene with the layers of paper it was wrapped in, and laid it on the commode lid that was in the corner stall. I tied a string to it that I was using for a wick. The string dropped down to the floor. I lit the end of the string and quickly started for the door. As I looked back over my shoulder, I could see the glow of flames reflecting in a puddle of water on the concrete floor under the stall.

As I entered the hallway, I looked in every direction and there was no one. I looked down toward the south end of the hall. Then, in the morning sun's light I could see a certain young girl with long brown hair that was an office worker coming from the secondary building, about to enter the main building. I was taking long fast steps toward my classroom. I sensed that the girl either didn't see me, or just wasn't paying any attention.

As I eased back into the room, I took my seat and whispered to shane, *"I did it."*

Probably, about fifteen minutes later, as Mrs. Graves was lecturing, she seemed to be distracted by some activity in the hallway. Then, she left the room. She came back in and said to us, "Someone just went into the boys bathroom and set the commode lid on fire."

When she said this, the whole class roared with laughter.

The commode lid was practically destroyed. Everyone wanted to go and see it. The girls wanted to see it. I don't remember if they let them see it or not. The bathroom became a museum of sorts.

As we were headed to fourth period class, Mr. Ralston was standing in the hall. Shane said to him something to the effect, "Mr. Ralston, someone set the commode lid on fire and burned it up." He said this as if he didn't already know. He (Mr. Ralston) stood in the hallway with what seemed to me at the time, to be a puzzled expression on his face.

That afternoon during recess, Mrs. Cannon met me in the hall. I don't remember what she was talking to me about, but she put her arm around my neck and we walked up the hall together. What she was talking to me about was pertaining to all the destruction that had been done in the school. She was talking very nice to me, and I could tell from her demeanor, that she didn't suspect me. She, and all the other teachers seemed mystified about who would have set the bathroom on fire.

Right after this, I learned that when Daniel Packard left the bathroom in the beginning of third period, that he went to Mrs. Cannon's class. When it was known that someone had set the commode lid on fire, he had said to her, I saw Robert Massingill in the bathroom at the beginning of third period."

She asked him, "Does he smoke?"

Either himself or someone else said, "No."

Actually, I chewed tobacco. I don't know what that had to do with anything except to say that maybe someone who smoked would be more prone to carry matches than someone who didn't.

Smoking was allowed at school. But there was a designated area that it had to be done in. At the north area behind the main building was the smoking tree. Everybody who smoked had to smoke under the tree. But I didn't have to go to the tree to chew tobacco. I chewed it everywhere. I remember once in P.E. class, when Mr. Graves walked into the office that was in the back of the gym, he said to me, "I'm gonna sit down and have me a cigarette. You want one?"

I replied, "Naw, I've got tobacco today."

Shane asked me, "Did Daniel Packard see you in the bathroom?"

I answered, "Yeah, but that was in the beginning of third period. That don't mean nothing."

Apparently, I had them all fooled. That is, except for one person who eyed me suspiciously. That was Leon Garrett. As we were standing around in our study hall room, he said something to me to the effect, that he had me figured out.

I was carrying a brown nose drop bottle in my pocket that had either gasoline or kerosene in it. After he said what he did to me, he turned his back and walked away. When no one was looking, I eased over to the window and threw the bottle out on the ground.

That afternoon, I went into the bathroom to look at the commode lid like everybody else was doing. There were two or three guys standing around. One of them pointed at me jokingly, saying, "There's the one who done it."

I chuckled, saying, "No, I didn't either."

That afternoon on the school bus, several of us were talking about the incident. Stanley North said to me when he heard about it, "They'll find out who did it. Somebody'll get mad at somebody and tell on'em, or somebody'll be talking about it or something."

I agreed with him saying, something like, "Yeah, they probably will."

A few days later, Josh Watson and I were discussing who left the room during third period. He asked me something to the effct, "Who all went outta the room?"

I replied, "I went and got me a drink one time, but that's all."

They were aware that Shane and I were capable of pranks such as stealing library labels, or taking screws out of the radiator. But apparently, they could not connect it to setting the bathroom on fire.

It reminds me a little bit like tracking a serial killer. For instance, the night stalker. He always struck at night. For a while, he wore the same shoes. He used the same weapon. That is, until he found out what they were looking for and threw them over the Golden Gate Bridge.

But what if the serial killer, who in the past, had left people dead without taking their money, decided to rob the bank? Then take the money and leave everyone alive and unharmed? The patterns start to cross each other and run together. He becomes harder to track.

In a way, what the teachers were seeing in me was the tip of the iceburg. But not really. They were seeing a glimpse of the tip of the tip of the iceburg. I don't know about Shane, but when they were dealing with me, they had not the slightest idea what they were dealing with.

One day in homeroom class, Ralph French and I were talking about the situation concerning the commode lid being burnt. He was conveying to me that whoever it was, had to be very smart. He said to me, "I know you didn't do it. You're not smart enough. You'd have got caught."

I agreed with him, saying, "Yeah, I know it. If I'd done it, there would've come Mrs. Cannon walking right in. Then, I'd have got caught."

There were a few times, that neither I, nor Shane were involved in certain capers. One morning in math class, Mr. Madison walked in and said threateningly, "The next time someone's caught breaking in the gym, they're gonna be prosecuted!" I don't recall who it was, but two or three boys were caught breaking into the gym that morning. I never knew the exact details, but they were dealt with by Mrs. Cannon.

Every classroom had an intercom system that was connected to the office. The principal, or any other office worker could make announcements to the whole school at one time.

Someone went around to certain rooms and cut the wires that ran from the intercom to the office.

One day when I was in the line at the lunchroom, Mrs. Cannon approached me, calling me over to the side. As she stood there with her note pad ready to write, she asked me, "What are your reasons for saying that Shane cut those wires?"

I replied, "I never did say that he did."

"Oh," she said, "There must've been a misunderstanding. I heard that you were saying that Shane did that."

I said, "Yeah, there must've been a rumor that got started somehow."

By coincidence, the day the wires were discovered cut, Shane wasn't at school; he was absent that day. Mr. Monahan paid one of our classes a friendly visit. As he sat behind the desk, he asked, "Where's my friend, Shane Sinclair?"

Someone said, "He's out today."

He said something to the effect, "Out today, huh? Well, okay."

It was not unusual for him to visit our classes, especially when Shane was involved. Not only Shane, but he would have friendly conversations with different students a lot of times when he came around. For instance, on one occasion, Mrs. Graves took the class on a field trip. Right after the field trip, he was visiting our classroom. As he was sitting behind the desk holding a fishing cane, Shane asked him, "Mr. Monahan, what would you say if I told you that I drunk a co-cola? (We were not allowed to drink cokes unless it was recess.)

He replied, "I'd wear one of these canes out on you."

Then, Shane asked, "What would you say if I told you that I drunk two co-colas?"

Then, he replied smoothly, "I'd wear two of these canes out on you."

Then he asked, "What would you say if I told you I drunk six?"

"I'd whip you for lying," he replied.

Then, Shane explained that we had been on a field trip, and he came back hot and thirsty. So, under the circumstances, Mr. Monahan replied, "Well, that's different."

When Shane returned to school the next day, I told him that Mr. Monahan had asked about him. Shane replied, "Well, since I wasn't here, he knows I couldn't be the one who cut the wires."

There were other occasions when someone paid the school house a visit, and broke out a lot of windows. Apparently, it must have been done either at night, or sometime before or after school. As far as I remember, they never knew who did it. I remember on one occasion early in the morning when I had just got to school, when I discovered that several windows at the secondary building had been busted. There were three new boys who had just started to our school. Two of them were about my height and the other was tall with brownish or blonde hair. They were standing at the south end of the main building. I approached them and asked, "Do you'all wanna see something funny?" I don't recall exactly what their response was, but they followed me around the end of the building where the busted windows were.

One day in Mr. Graves's health class, he was admonishing the class concerning doing the right thing and not getting into meanness. In effect, he was saying that getting into meanness was not the answer to problems in life. Then he said emphatically, "Don't set the commode seat on fire."

There were three guys that were in the ninth grade, named Rod Chambers, Eric Phillips, and Dan Garner. Rod Chambers, who had brown hair, was heavy set and a little taller than Shane or myself. Eric Phillips was slim and taller. Dan Garner was about mine or Shane's size, maybe a little heavier. We were well acquainted with them. Sometimes, we got along with them all right. But sometimes, we might say something to them that they didn't like, or they might not like the way we said it, and they might get mad at us. Occasionally, Dan and I would wrestle around a little. It never amounted to anything. One time, we were scuffling, and I tripped him and caused him to fall down. It made him a little mad, but it never amounted to much.

One afternoon, just before the buses ran, Dan and I were scuffling around next to where the buses stopped. He was chasing me and slid down in a patch of grass. At the same time Eric had just got on his bus and had the window down. I don't know where Dan got the idea, but he hollered at Eric and said, "He's a spy," as he pointed at me.

Eric looked out the window of the bus as it passed by, and hollered at me threateningly, "I'll get you tomorrow."

Whatever gave them the idea that I was spying on them, I'll never know. But Shane was tied up in it too, since he and I were so close. As far as I know, they thought both of us were spies.

This created a fued between us. We tried to convince them that we were not spies. But they did not believe us. Shane and I were discussing this one day and he said to me, "If they tell you that they're the ones that burnt the commode lid you'll know they're trying to frame you."

The irony was: here I was the ring leader of destruction, and they thought I was a spy.

One day, Shane and I were sitting in our seats in our study hall room. Then, Jody Coltrane approached us, and said quietly, "There's someone out in the hall wanting to see you'all."

We asked him, "Who is it?"

He replied, "Eric Phillips."

Shane looked at me with a disgusted expression on his face, and said something like, "Now what?"

We went out into the hall and talked to them. I don't remember what they said to us, but they were threatening us, because they continued to believe we were spies.

Things got so bad, that I duscussed this with Mrs. Cannon, and told her what was going on. One afternoon, during recess, we were in a certain classroom next to the windows talking and I said to her, "A story got told that I smuggled a note to you."

Her mouth gasped open in shock as she took the last swallow from her coke bottle. Then, she replied, "You need to tell them that you've got enough problems of your own, without getting messed up in all this."

They finally figured out that we were not spies. I don't remember what opened their eyes, but they came up to us in the study hall room one day and said, "Hi."

One morning before school, right after they found out we were not spies, Josh Watson, Eric, and myself were in the bathroom at the lower left wing, talking. Eric said to us, "You'all know who burnt the commode lid?"

We asked, "Who?"

He pointed to himself, saying, "Me."

Josh looked at me with a bright look in his face, "Now, we know who did it."

I replied, "Yeah."

Then, he replied, "Naw, I was just joking. Don't you'all tell nobody I said that."

Right after these things, I went on a rampage to destroy every school book I could. Ordinarily, everybody was assigned their individual books, and at the end of the year, we turned them back in. If we did not have them to turn back in, he had to pay for them. But for some reason, they became lax in this. It got to where when we went to class, we just grabbed a book. If it was english class, science, or whatever class it was. I would take my books home in the afternoon, and they never returned to the school.

Down in the woods below our house, there was a small branch. I started taking the books to the creek, ripping the pages out of them, and throwing them into the creek. Day after day, I took two, three, four, or as many as I could get away with home with me. Then, I took them down to the creek. I took my anger out on them and left the pieces laying in the muddy creek bed. I counted fifty books of various subjects that went into the creek. I remember the red lettering from the front cover of a speech book that filtered through the crystal clear water as it lay on the bottom of the creek. Then, there was another fifty that I either burned in the stove, (we had a coal heater that we heated with) or buried in the ground.

The school had purchased some brand new english books, and some new spelling books. Many of those english books went home with me and never returned. I carried a razor blade with me a lot of times, and when no one was looking, I would slice up the new spelling books. One day, I was cutting up a spelling book, and Josh was sitting in front of me. Suddenly, he turned around and caught me cutting up the book. His eyes got rather big as a shocked expression came across his face. I told him not to tell anybody, and as far as I know, he never did.

One day, a certain girl with lengthy red hair came up to me and asked to borrow my science book. When I approached her later to get my book, she said to me, "This is my book. It's got my name on it."

"Oh, okay," I said, walking away feeling a little embarrassed. That was one book that didn't make it to the creek.

One day, we were in sixth period english class. Mr. Ralston had left to go get the school bus, and as always, we were left on our own. Shane and I were sitting in the back of the aisle, next to the inner wall, opposite from the windows. All of the others were either talking, or standing around. Shane asked me, "Do you think I can sneak over to the window and throw out a book without anybody seeing me?"

I said "No, you'd better not. That's too risky."

He said, "Yeah, I believe I will."

I said, "No, don't do it. Somebody'll see you." I tried and tried to talk him out of it, but to no avail.

He eased out of his seat with a book, then over to the window. He stood with his back to the window, and pushed the book out the window. Then, he eased back over to his seat. No one seemed to have noticed what he did. Then, he asked me, "Do you think I can do another one?"

Again, I tried to get him not to do it. "I said something to the effect, "No, don't do it, you might get caught."

Again, he eased out of his seat and over to the window. He backed up to the window, as before. Then like before, he pushed the book out the window. Behind him, I could see the edges of the book going over the ledge. One was a new english book. The other was a reader's digest.

Now, the room we were in was on the south section of the main building on the west side. Directly behind the building was the woodworking shop hosted by Mr. Vining. And also connected to it was the band room. The band teacher was a tall, dark haired man, named, Mr. Palance.

After a few minutes, he (Mr. Palance) stuck his head through the door, and we heard a deep voice asking, "Who threw that book out the window?"

A certain blonde headed girl standing on the other side of the room, remembered noticing Shane sneaking over to the window. Then, she pointed an accusing finger at him, and exclaimed, "Shane, you did that."

Mr. Palance and the others looked at Shane suspiciously, as he replied something to the effect, "Mr. Ralston's gonna be upset if someone don't admit it."

But we argued that it couldn't have been Shane, because he was sitting on the other side of the room.

As Mr. Ralston was questioning the class the next day, Tony

Shield's (he is the same Tony Shields I knew at Atcooga years before) said to Mr. Ralston, "Shane was sitting over there in that corner."

The next morning, we were in Mr. Madison's math class. He was lecturing about the daily lesson when he suddenly said to Shane, "Sinclair, go to the office." Shane got up and went to the office. They had called him to the office concerning the books that he threw out the window.

Later that day, Shane was asked by the other students, "Did you throw that book out the window?"

He responded, "I ain't saying."

The story was, that he had admitted to doing it and made arrangements to pay for the books.

Now, about the library labels. He admitted to Mrs. Cannon that we stole the library labels.

One Friday afternoon, Leon Garrett and I were sitting in the back of our study hall room, talking. Mrs. Cannon walked up to us and discussed something with Leon. Then, she said to me, "I wanna see you Monday."

Although I wouldn't let Leon in on what I was doing, he and I were good friends. We also stuck together on certain issues. For instance, they came up with a rule, that when we were in the lunch room, we had a certain amount of time to eat, and then, we would have to go back to class whether we were through eating or not. On one occasion Shane asked Mr. Ralston, "What if we're not through eating?"

He responded, "Shovel it down, and then, get down here."

I remember one day, Leon, myself, and several others were eating at a table. One of the girls came over to us and replied, "Mrs. Lansing said for you'all to come on."

Leon defiantly responded, "Oh, no, we won't, till we're through eating." And we all took our time and finished eating.

When I went to see Mrs. Cannon that Monday, she informed me that Shane had told her that we took the labels from the library. She questioned me concerning any trouble I had been into when I was in the elementary school. I beat around the bush with her, saying, "I may've got in trouble once in a while." But I didn't tell her anything specific. I was also uncertain of what all Shane had told her. He had told me once, that he had told her everything I did over there. But since she did not confront me with anything specific, I figured that he must not have. So I agreed to help Shane pay for the labels. But apparently, she was not aware of all the destruction I was actually responsible for.

During our conversation, she mentioned the situation about the commode lid being burnt, but not implying that I was a suspect. She was conveying the idea that they intended to find out who did it. I said, "I didn't do that now."

She replied something to the effect, "Oh, I know you didn't do that."

One afternoon during english class, after Mr. Ralston had left, Shane and I were discussing these things. He said to me, "You'd go to reform school if they knew how many books you tore up."

I replied, "Yeah, I know."

Then, he looked up toward the shelf in the corner and spied the english book that he had thrown out the window. It had a large mud stain on it. Then, he said, "I paid for that book, and their not keeping it." He got the book off the shelf and took it home.

The next day he said to me, "I went for a walk yesterday, and I found a big mud hole, and I threw that book in it."

Not long after these things, I plotted to burn another commode lid. I took a tube of gasoline as before, and wrapped it in notebook paper. But this time I did something different. I took a 410 gage shotgun shell apart, took the lead out of it, and put in it a double charge of powder.

Every afternoon after school, unless it was very cold, they made everybody go outside and stay out of the building. There was a period of about ten minutes or so, then, there would be

99

three bells that would ring. When the bells rang, everyone had to go outside. There was always a teacher on hall duty. They all took turns. The one on hall duty would walk the hall like a guard, and keep everyone out of the hall.

One afternoon, I sneaked into the bathroom right after school. I managed to elude the teacher that was on hall duty. It was the same bathroom I burnt the commode lid in before, and the same commode. I set it on fire the same way and left the building. I went all the way around the building and entered the front entrance. I was walking down the hall toward the lower left wing, (where I had just set the fire) as the three final bells rang. I remember seeing Mrs. Cannon walking down the hall. The best I recall, she was very close to where the fire was set. Right in the middle of the second ring, I heard the shotgun shell explode. Then, I walked back outside and stayed.

Strangely enough, the fire did very little damage to the commode lid. We could see where the fire scorched it. I figured when the shell exploded, it scattered the fire.

The next day, I didn't hear much said about it. In retrospect, I figure they were keeping quiet, hoping somebody would say something that would give them a lead.

One day during P.E. class, we were picking up paper around the gym. There next to the front, under some rocks, I discovered a water cut-off. It was a wheel valve. I turned it off and left it. Then, it was discovered that there was no water in the bathrooms that were in the front of the gym. I didn't tell anybody but Shane about the cut-off. For about a month the water stayed off. Since no one ever turned it back on, I assumed that Mr. Madison or Mr. Graves, nor anyone else knew it was there.

Then, one sunny day during P.E. class, we were all out there. On this occasion, Mr. Madison had the gym locked to keep everyone out.

This was not unusual. There were times that he would have the floor waxed or something and didn't want anyone on the floor. There was a certain occasion when he had it locked with the floors waxed. Our class came out there and found it locked. Then, Shane climed up on the back of the building, went in through an open window and opened the door. (I also followed right behind him.) Then, Mr. Madison came out there and found everyone running around on his waxed floor.

He was furious at Shane for opening the door. He chewed him out, and told him that what he did was considered breaking an entry. However, in this particular instance, Mr. Graves had a different reaction. That same afternoon he met Shane and I in the hall and replied to Shane as he chortled, "Boy, the coach really got on to you this morning didn't he?" Then, he asked him, "What'n the Sam Hill was you doing on the gym floor anyway?"

Then, I spoke up saying in a joking like manner, "He wasn't on it; he opened the door and they got on it." It was sort of amazing to me that after Mr. Madison reacting angrily about it they way he did that Mr. Graves chortled about it in this manner. But I enjoyed every minute of it.

Again, on this particular morning, the gym was locked. They had all the class out in front where the picnic area was, doing some work. In the process of things, Shane and I were fooling around in front of the gym. He found the wheel valve and turned it back on. I said to him, "Cut that back off, I don't want them to have no water in the front of the gym."

Then, he walked around and looked in the front window, and said to me, "Robert, commere."

I walked around and peered through the window (we both had to tiptoe to look through) as the sun's rays reflected off the glass. As I adjusted my eyes, I could see a sink rapidly filling with water. Then I changed my mind and told him to leave it on.

Then, we walked out to where everybody else was, and acted natural. We were lifting a heavy pole of some sort, and I remember Mr. Madison saying to me, "Grab that, Massingill."

As the end of second period approached, everyone headed to the front of the gym. As far as I recall, they had left their books and things on the floor of the gym.

I remember a certain blonde headed girl exclaiming, "The gym! It's flooded!"

Everyone ran through the front doors in haste to find the floor covered with water. Mr. Madison was furious. Several people worked a half a day mopping water.

The next day in math class, Mr. Madison and some of the boys were debating how whoever that did it got inside to do it. There was no evidence of forced entry. The door was locked. It hadn't been picked that they could tell.

Mr. Madison angrily replied, "There was over a hundred gallons of water on that floor."

The next day, at the end of second period, Shane and I were sitting on the picnic tables under the shed, when Leon Garrett ran up to us and asked, "Did you'all flood the gym again today?"

I answered, "We didn't flood it yesterday."

He replied, "Yeah, you'all did."

We continued to deny it. I will always believe that Mr. Madison suspected us of doing it. The problem was, he just couldn't figure out how.

A few days later, I was at the trash pile behind the gym. I don't remember what I was supposed to be doing there, but I was piddling around, pouring coal tar all over a big water tank that had been thrown away. Mr. Madison approached me and asked, "Robert did you'll see anyone messing around the gym that morning it was flooded?"

I answered, "No, we didn't."

I sensed from the tone of his voice, that he suspected us. And also, the fact that he called me by my first name. That told me something was wrong.

Along about this time, I decided to send a letter to Mr. Monahan, and not let him know who I was. Inside the letter, I enclosed two or three torn pages from a school book, and told him that they were part of many books that I had destroyed.

(Now, I had nothing against him personally, but since he was the principal, he was caught in the middle.) I told him that I was the one who burned the commode lid and many other destructive things done in the school. I disguised the handwriting to where I didn't think he could trace it. I did not mail the letter myself, I arranged for it to be mailed from somewhere in Dalton. I didn't want it mailed from our home mailbox. I was afraid they might be able to trace it somehow. I never knew if he got it or not, but in the letter I was laughing in their face.

My war against the school continued. But as God and Satan were engaging in warfare over me, God had a roadblock prepared that lay somewhere up ahead that would eventually bring the war unto it's final conclusion.

CHAPTER SEVEN
DEATH STRUGGLE

The year ended and I went to the ninth grade. The war I waged against the school continued, but it was not as intense as it was the year before.

We were under a new restriction concerning the school books. Because of so many books disappearing, we were told that before we could get our report cards at the end of the year, or go to the next grade, we would have to account for all of our school books.

My homeroom teacher was an elderly lady with dark reddish hair, named Mrs. Hallberg.

My first period class was algebra, with Mrs. Stanley, a young lady with brownish colored hair. She was a very friendly lady, and treated everybody nice. She was a lot like my seventh grade english teacher, Mrs. Cooper.

I was intimated with algebra. I told myself that I couldn't learn it. Mr. Madison had taught us algebra in the eighth grade, in an attempt to prepare us for the ninth grade. But I sat on the back seat all year and failed it.

There were many times, that I pretended to be stupid. I would just act silly. It was all an act, but I would lead people to believe that I was about half crazy. One morning, Mrs. Stanley had written the daily assignment on the blackboard. Everyone was supposed to be copying it. There were two boys named, Roland, and Cecil, that sat close to me. They both had brownish hair and Roland was a little taller than Cecil. As I was sitting idle, Cecil said to me, "Robert, go erase the board." He said this, just to see if I was crazy enough to do it. So, I walked up front and began to erase the board.

Mrs. Stanley looked around at me, and in a surprised tone of voice, asked me, "What're you doing?"

I replied, "They told me to erase the board."

Then she said, "Go sit down, Robert." Then she turned to the class and said, "You'all be careful what you'all tell this boy to do."

My second period class was agriculture, with Mr. Vining, a slim, elderly man with thinning hair. In the beginning, I was interested in learning about wood working and the things this class had to offer.

My third period class was science. I was in Mr. Bailey's class. He was a tall, heavy built man with graying hair. Science was one of the easiest subjects I had. I could have passed it easily. But for reasons I still wonder about, I sat there all year and failed it anyway.

Although I failed it, there were times that I gave some input. For instance, on a test once, one of the questions were, "Which has the longest needles, the long leaf pine, or the short leaf pine?" I got that one right.

Mr. Bailey was easy to get along with. That is, as long as we didn't disturb the class. Different teachers had different ways of dealing with different situations. He was one of those teachers that allowed you to piddle around and do nothing, as long as you didn't disturb other students.

My fourth period class was P.E. Since I was so good about cleaning up and sweeping the floor, Mr. Madison let me sweep the floor all year instead of dressing out and doing exercises. At the end of the year, he gave me a unit just as if I had done P.E.

I hung around by myself a lot, that is, when I wasn't with Shane. He and I still hung out together. One of the reasons I volunteered to clean up the gym, was so that I could be alone. There was a heavy set boy with dark hair named Brent, that moved from another state, and started coming to our school. He, Shane, and I got to be friends. He, like many others could not understand why I always cleaned up the gym. He asked me once, "Why do you always clean up the joint?"

I replied, "Because I want to."

My fifth period class was english, hosted by a tall, dark headed lady named Mrs Caldwell. She was probably in her early thirties. She was a good teacher, and easy to get along with. Like Mrs. Lansing, people liked to aggravate her, to hear her gripe and yell at them.

Early one morning, Josh Watson and I were walking up the sidewalk behind the building, beside Mrs. Caldwell's classroom. Then, he looked down and spied a dirty looking white sock laying on the ground. One of the windows to her classroom happened to be partly opened. He picked up the sock and hung it over the frame of the window. But because of the reflection, neither of us noticed that she was in her room, sitting behind her desk. Then, she came to the window and yelled sharply, "Josh Watson!" He walked over to the window, and she handed him the sock.

My sixth period class was spanish. I was fascinated with foreign languages. If there ever was a subject that I was interested in, it was spanish. The teacher was Miss Moore, a young dark haired lady probably in her thirties. She wasn't as tall as Mrs. Caldwell; she was shorter. She was a good teacher, and she liked me.

During my seventh year, I had a teacher in spelling class, named, Miss Connors. She was young, slim, with long dark hair. She knew spanish, and used to teach us spanish words. But one day, I asked her how to say dinosaur in spanish. She didn't seem to know what I was talking about.

One day, Rod Chambers and I were sitting in the office in the back of the gym, discussing the subjects we took. I was sharing with him that I was taking spanish. He replied, "What'd you take that for? That's too hard."

Leon Garrett sat in front of me, and Shane sat behind me. Miss Moore was different from Mr. Bailey. She would not allow some of the things that he would. Every day in class, Leon would lay his head down and go to sleep. Mr. Bailey

107

would have allowed that. She would wake him up and make him study and pay attention. She was not about to let someone sit in her class and sleep all period long.

One day when he was asleep, she woke him up and tried to get him to study. He did not have his book with him, so she was going to let him use hers. He woke up and started snapping at her, saying something to the effect, "I don't get to sleep much at night, now leave me alone!"

She said to him, "Hush." She told him that he could not stay in her class and sleep. She took him with her and they left the room for a few minutes.

He came back into the room and replied to Shane and I, "Well, I'm getting outta here." So he left and went to another class.

In science class, Shane and I, and a boy a little taller than we were, named John Windoms all three sat next to each other. We sat next to the back, one behind another. Shane sat in front of me, and John sat behind me.

One day, Shane and John got into a playful fist fight. They were standing up in their seats, swinging over my head as I lay low in my seat.

About that time, Mr. Bailey shouted at them; Shane! John! and then he said, "Come up here." He had a strange way of discipline. I remember once, when he made a boy get down on his hands and knees, and hold his head in the desk all period. He said to them, "Both of you lay here in the floor for the rest of the period."

At first, Shane refused to do it. He (Mr. Bailey) told him he was going to go call his parents if he did not comply with this. As he started toward the door to go call, Shane said, "All right, I'll do it this time."

They lay there all period. Every chance I got, I would point and make fun of them.

One morning, Mr. Bailey passed out the weekly readers, which was part of our lesson for the day. After we all had left his class, he looked out and spied three weekly readers laying on the ground. They were laying beside the windows, next to where the three of us had been sitting.

The next day, he shared with us about where he had seen our weekly readers. Then he told us that we could go outside and pick up paper all period. Shane happened to be absent from school that day, so John and I spent third period picking up paper.

One morning, when I got on the school bus, I walked down the aisle as always, in an attempt to find a seat. The bus was fairly loaded and there weren't many seats left. There was a boy named Norman Price, who had moved into our neighborhood sometime before this. Himself and another person were sitting in a certain seat near the back, and I started to sit in the seat next to him. But as I started to sit down, he resisted me and replied stiffly, "This seat's saved."

So, I started to sit in another seat across the aisle but further toward the back, and the person sitting there said, "This seat's saved."

When the person said that, Norman looked around and said to me in a ridgid tone of voice, "That's seat's saved!"

So far, I had not made any comment, but when he said that, I retorted to him, "You think I don't know it? I'll knock you through that door in a minute!"

Now, Norman was two years older than I was, and also a lot bigger. I probably weighed about 135 pounds. He was taller and dark headed, weighing about 200. This incident created a feud between us that lasted for quite some time.

Every Halloween night, the kids always went trick or treating. This particular year, I devised a plot to break into the school.

As we all went out into the roads of the neighborhood, it would usually get wild. Sometimes, there would be firecracker throwing, egg throwing and no telling what.

DIAGRAM 4
CAMPUS LAYOUT

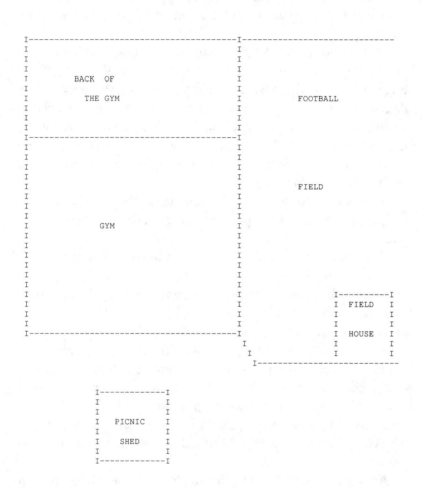

DIAGRAM 5
AREA OVERVIEW

```
  I   I                                                      H  I  I
  I   I                                                      I  I  I
  I   I                                                      G  I  I
  I   I                                                      H  I  I
  I   I                                                      W  I  I
  I   I                                                      A  I  I
-----------------------------------------------------------------I--I--
  I   I  SOUTHERN      RAILROAD                              Y  I  I
-----------------------------------------------------------------I--I--
  I   I                                                         I  I
  I   I                                                      4  I  I
  I   I                                                      1  I  I
  I   I                                                         I  I
-------------------------------------------------------------I   I  I
  I   I                  DIRT ROAD                          I   I  I
---------------------------------------------------------I I--I I  I  I
  I C I                                         OLD  I  I    I  I I  I
  I R I                                         ROAD I  I    I  II  I
  I E I                                              I  I    I      I
  I E I                                              I  I    I      I
  I K I                                              I  I    I      I
  I   I                              I------------------I    I      I
 I   I                               I                  I    I      I
 I   I                               I   BACK OF        I    I      I
 I   I                               I                  I    I      I
 I   I                               I   GYM            I    I      I
 I   I                               I                  I    I      I
 I   I                               I------------------I    I      I
 I   I   SEC          MAIN           I                  I    I      I
 I   I   I----I    I----------I      I                  I    I      I
 I   I   I    I    I  BLDG    I      I                  I    I      I
 I   I   I    I    I          I      I   GYM            I    I      I
 I   I   I----I    I----------I      I                  I    I      I
 I   I   BLDG                        I                  I    I      I
 I   I                               I                  I    I      I
 I   I                               I                  I    I      I
 I   I                               I                  I    I      I
 I   I                               I------------------I    I      I
 I   I                                                       I      I
 I   I                                                       I      I
 I   I                                                       I      I
 I   I                                                       I      I
 I   I                                                       I      I
 I   I                                                       I      I
 I   I                                                       I      I
 I   I                                                       I      I
 I   I                                                       I      I
 I   I                                                       I      I
 I   I                                                       I      I
 I   I                                                       I      I
 I   I                                                       I      I
```

111

I threw a quilt over my head and stole away from the crowd. The school was a good five miles away. Less than a mile from our house, I passed in front of John Windoms's house. He came out to the road and discovered who I was. He asked me a bunch of questions. He wondered why I wasn't with my family, and the other neighbors. I finally got away from him and kept going. I came to the railroad crossing at Five Springs Road, and then headed down the railroad tracks. The Southern Railroad and the L&N ran side by side. But a half a mile or so down, they separated. The L&N turned and went toward Tilton. The Southern continued straight south and went right behind the high school. Between the railroad tracks and the school, there was a dirt road. From the dirt road to the back of the gym, there was a road cut through the woods wide enough for a car to pass through.

There was a creek that ran east and west, and ran under the railroad, and the dirt road. Then, it ran south of the school and ran under forty-one highway. Oftentimes, we would sneak off from school, and go down there and explore. We used to drink out of it. That is, until one day we were following it upstream, and discovered that it forked off. One side of it was white, milky looking chemical mixing in with the clear water. Then, we never drank out of it again.

North of the school, there was an overhead bridge where the railroad went under the highway.

I crossed through the weeds from the railroad to the dirt road. Then, in the darkness I walked up the little road to the back of the gym. I walked behind the back of the gym, and I'll never forget how deftly quiet it seemed. I walked up behind the north end of the main building. Then, I discovered a window of the girl's bathroom that wasn't locked. I opened it and climbed inside the bathroom into the darkness. I eased the door open and the lights were all on in the hall. Then, I climbed back outside. There was a thick door mat that lay in front of the back entrance of the north left wing, next to the cafeteria. I drug it down into the woods and left it.

I walked down toward the south end of the building. When I got to the lower left wing, I discovered that the door was ajar. I peered through the window, and it appeared that someone was in there working. It seemed like I saw an electric cord running through the classroom door that was across the hall.

Although I never actually saw anyone, but being that it appeared to me that someone was inside, I left and headed back home. About 11.00 P.M., I arrived in front of Stanley North's house. There, I met my youngest sister, Dorothy, and Stanley's older sister, Beverly. They were standing under the shadows of the large oak trees, talking.

The next morning on the bus, the kids in the neighborhood were talking about all the fun they had the night before. From the way they talked, they were unaware that I wasn't among the crowds running in the roads.

At school the next morning, myself and some other people were standing around behind the building at the north left wing. Mrs. Hallberg came out to check on all of us. Then, she said to us, "Where's the mat out here?"

Sometime later, John Windoms accused me of having it with me when I passed by his house. He thought that was what I had over my head. He said to me, "That's what that was."

There was a certain boy named Randall Morris, a little taller than I was, whom I had been friends with, since elementary. Early one cold morning, I was hanging around the south end of the building, as I always did. (When it was cold, they would let us go inside to a study hall room if we wanted to. But I always stayed outside regardless of how cold it was. Once, Mr. Vining asked me why I always stayed outside in the cold. I don't remember what I told him, but I had the attitude that I wasn't going in as long as I wasn't forced to. I hated the school so bad, that I would freeze before I would go in voluntarily.) He approached me and asked me to play hookey with him. Since no one had seen me except a boy about my size, named Wayne Mathis, I decided to go with him. (Wayne said he wouldn't tell anybody.)

Playing hookey was something that I rarely ever did. However, there were a couple of times that I did. On one such occasion in the seventh grade, I hid out in the woods on a cloudy day. It was on a Monday. The next day, Mr. Todd asked me why I was out. I told him I was sick. There had been times before this that he had advised the class that we shouldn't stay out of school so often. He believed that people were not as sick as much as they claimed to be. Then, making eye contact with me, he replied, "You'all are not as sick as much as you're out."

Then, when he left the room, Leon Garrett turned around and asked me, "Now, where'd you play hookey at?" Everybody heard him, and then, turned toward me and started grinning.

We followed the railroad tracks about a mile north and went to a guy's house that Randall knew. The guy's name was Nolen, a brownish haired boy a little bigger than we were. Apparently, he was old enough to quit school. He was home alone. We stayed there most of the day and played poker. (We were not gambling; we played with buttons just for funs.)

Later that afternoon, we went to Randall's house. His aunt, a short, dark haired, middle aged lady was there. When she saw us coming into the house, she asked demandingly, "What're you doing home?" She continued to yell at him, threatening to tell his daddy about him not being at school.

But he responded to her and said to the effect, "Oh, you don't know what you're talking about. He won't believe you anyway." Later, I went on home.

There was a slim, light brown headed boy, named Eddie Perkins that we were friends with. Sometime after this, the three of us played hookey together. We went to Nolen's house and played poker as before.

The next day, Shane asked me, "Where was you at yesterday?"

I said something to the effect, "I was out yesterday."

Then he replied sarcastically, "I bet your mama and daddy

didn't know where you was at; and I bet Randall Morris's mama and daddy didn't know where he was at, and I bet Eddie Perkins's mama and daddy didn't know where he was at."

On another cold winter morning during this time, Randall talked me in to going with him again. We were down at the creek behind the school, and the temperature was below freezing. Randall was wearing a pair of black combat boots. Shortly, he stepped on a piece of wood at the edge of the creek, and his foot slipped. He ran his foot into the creek over his boot. He pulled his foot out of the water and exclaimed, "My foot's freezing!"

We went to his house and hid behind the barn so his aunt wouldn't see us. We climbed up the back wall of the barn, and climbed inside. We stayed there almost all day. Then, finally we decided to take a chance on going into the house. There was a dirt road between the barn and the house. So we crossed the road to the front yard. Then, as we passed through the shade of a large oak tree, he said, "I can tell if she's in there or not." He threw a snowball into the house and bounced it off the living room door. (It was a sunshinny day, but there was snow still on the ground from a recent snow.) He said if she was in there, she would come out yelling. But she wasn't there. Then, we figured out that she had not been there all day.

Now, the slaughter house was located between the elementary building and the high school building, toward the south of the campus. It was connected to the same building where the old lunch room was a few years earlier. A lot of times, Randall's daddy worked there. Sometimes, we would go over there before school in the mornings. One morning, the three of us met there to discuss the next time we should play hookey. I said to them, "We should wait about two weeks." I had this instinctive feeling that we were doing it too often.

Eddie looked at me with a disagreeing expression on his face and exclaimed, "Two weeks?"

They said that they were going that day. So I went on to

school.

Before school that morning, Shane, myself, and some others were hanging around the south end of the building, when Shane bent over too far and busted the seat of his breeches. He had to go sew up his paints. Between this and a lot of other things that were happening, I forgot all about Randall and Eddie.

Sometime in the middle of the day, I went into the principal's office for something. When I walked in, I noticed Eddie sitting there on the couch. At first, I didn't think anything about it. I said to him, "Howdy Eddie."

Then he replied, "Howdy, Massingill."

I walked out into the hall, and then it hit me. I remembered that they played hookey that morning. I speedly walked down the hall and excitedly said to Shane, "Randall Morris and Eddie Perkins played hookey this morning and Eddie's in the office."

Shane tore out speedly up the hall, brushing by several people, then went into the office and asked Eddie what happened. Eddie explained that they had gone into a certain store that morning to get something to eat. Then they went to Nolen's. They believed that the store keeper had reported them. Mrs. Cannon pulled up in front of Nolen's house and got them. Eddie said, "She asked us, `Where's Robert?' We said, `He didn't come with us. He's at school.'" Then he said to me, "You're in the clear."

Later that day, Shane was on his way to the field house for something, and Mrs. Cannon met him in the hall and asked him, "Where's Robert?"

He answered, "He's headed to the field house, and I am too."

She said, "Tell him I wanna see him."

Then Shane found me and said, "Mrs. Cannon wants to see you."

I went to her room to see what she wanted with me. Then, she said to me, "Randall and Eddie layed out this morning."

I didn't come out and tell her that I knew it all the time, but I said, "Yeah", as if to give her the impression that I knew.

She said, "I checked to see if you were here today, and I sure was glad you were here." As I remember the incident, her intention was to admonish me not to yield to the temptation to play hookey.

The feud between Norman and I continued to intensify. There was always something happening between us. On one occasion, I was keeping some catfish in the branch below our house, and either he, or his brothers fished them out of the creek, and killed them. Then they left them laying beside the branch. There were countless times that we threathened each other on the school bus, badmouthed, and cussed each other.

One day, not long after they had killed the catfish, I was walking through the woods in the same vicinity. Then I met a couple of the neighborhood boys walking through the woods. It was Stanley North, and a boy, named Zackary Wilmington. Zackary was about three years younger than I was with lengthy, straight brown hair similiar to what the beetles wore. (At this time, I was about fourteen.) He had an older brother named Craig, who was about a year younger than I was.

Sometime before these things, Zackary, myself, and some of the other neighborhood kids were playing around at one of the neighbor's houses on a sunny day. Norman was there also. He and I were not speaking to each other. Somewhere in the course of this, Zackary said to us, "Why don't you two make up?"

Then, Norman spoke up and said firmly, "I don't make up with anybody I've got a grudge against." I made no reply.

They were carrying some homemade golf clubs. They told me that they had stolen them from Norman Price. I told them to give them to me, and they did. I broke them in pieces and left them in the trail where I figured Norman would see them.

One morning before school, a day or two later, I was hanging around outside the building at the lower left wing as always.

Then Norman angrily came through the door in a threathening attitude and asked demandingly to the effect, "Are you ready to pay for some golf clubs?"

Then I retorted, "Are you ready to pay for some catfish?"

Then, he said something like, "I'm gonna get you right now!"

He came at me, and I grabbed a nearby coke bottle, busted the bottom out of it, and as pieces of broken glass scattered all over the concrete porch, I exclaimed to him, using violent profanity, "I'll cut your guts out!"

As we both walked away from each other, he continued cussing and threatening me as he walked on away.

One sunny Saturday, Mike and I were burning trash behind the house among the wooded area. I had a habit of throwing pine straw on the fire, just to see it smoke. The more straw I could get on the fire, the more smoke it would make. We were running back and forth throwing straw on the fire. As I was throwing an arm load of straw on the fire, I fell face down in the trash pile. I subconsciously felt something hit my right wrist. As I got up, I glanced at my wrist, and saw that it was laid open. I could see the bones showing. I ran to the house leaving behind a trail of blood drops. Not realizing what had happened, Mike wondered why I suddenly ran toward the house. Daddy made a tourniquet to try to stop the flow of blood.

As we were on the way to the hospital in Daddy's black Ford, I held it to slow the bleeding as much as possible. He said to me, "Don't you pass out now." He shouldn't have said that. Then I started feeling swimmy headed, like I was going to pass out.

At the emergency room, *Doctor Wells was called in to sew it up. When he came into the room, I noticed that he didn't seem shakened. I figured that by him being a doctor, that to him this wasn't a serious injury. This made me feel more comfortable. He asked me something like, "How're you doing sport?"

I said something to the effect, "All right, I guess."

Then one of the nurses asked me, "Have you ever been sewed up before?"

I answered, "Yeah."

Then she responded, "Well, you know what your in for then."

Actually, I was mistaken. The reason I told her that I had been sewed up before, was that when I was in the hospital the year before with my leg, I was thinking that they sewed it up. But after *Dr. Whitfield drained out the poison, they put a butterfly bandage on it.

As he was sewing it up, he proclaimed smoothly, "Catgut on the needle." In retrospect, he reminded me of the T.V. actor, Pat Hingle.

I didn't look. Each time the needle went in, I imagined a concrete block pressing down on my wrist. For some reason, that softened the pain from the needle.

In the Old Testament book of Jonah, there is a story recorded about a man who disobeyed God. God told him to go in a certain direction, but he went in the opposite direction from where God told him to go. God sent him to Nineveh to proclaim His Word to them. But Jonah didn't want to, and he fled in the other direction. He went to Joppa, boarded a ship, and headed to a city called Tarshish. As the ship traveled out into the Mediterranean Sea, God sent a big storm into the sea. Jonah knew why the storm came. He told the people on the ship, the only way for the storm to go away, was to throw him into the sea. The men in charge of the ship didn't want to throw him into the sea. They tried to steer the ship out of the storm, but they could not. So then, they saw that they had no other choice. He was thrown into the sea and was swallowed by a great fish. Inside the fish, he repented and asked God to give him another chance. Then the fish vomited him up on the seashore.

God knows how to send storms into people's lives to get their attention, as it was in the case in my life.

That following Monday night, I went to bed. After I had lain down, there was suddenly a panic that came over me. I started tossing in the bed and yelling. Mama came into the bedroom to see what was wrong. Mama was about as nervous as I was, but Daddy wasn't shook up at all. He laughed, and said he was expecting it. When my wrist was cut, there were some nerves that were cut. Those nerves were beginning to heal. It usually took about three days, he said. He had seen it years before, when he was in the war. But because of my age, it didn't take hardly that long. It was only two and a half days.

But in my case, the problem was far more complicated than that. According to what he said, it should go away after a short time. But in my case, it didn't go away.

I could not lay on my back and sleep. I thought I couldn't breathe, and my chest felt like it was going to cave in. I had to position myself on my side a certain way to sleep. Constantly, I was terrified that my heart was going to stop. I thought I was dying. I constantly was thinking about death.

During all of this, I thought about God. I tried to comfort myself, by telling myself Bible stories about Adam and Eve. It seemed like the only cure for this thing was to get saved by praying to Jesus for forgiveness for my sins. I knew that if I did that, I wouldn't have any more trouble. I knew then, that I would go to heaven. So, in that situation, if I died, it wouldn't matter.

But I was caught between two or three things. At the time, I was under so much Satanic influence, that I thought I really could not live for God. I had it in my mind, that I could not live a Christian life until I got grown.

The days turned into weeks. The weeks turned into months. The months turned into years. I can remember times that I was sitting in class at school and feeling fear that my heart was going to stop.

One sunny afternoon, I was home alone. I was watching a soap opera. I don't remember what it was about, but there was this woman that either had, or thought she had something wrong with her brains. The people who were consoling her said to her, "There's nothing wrong with your brains."

When I heard this, I thought there was something wrong with my brains. Anytime I heard anything like this, I thought it was going to happen to me.

Once, I was reading a brochure about the ill effects of smoking. It was talking about emphysema. Then, although I didn't smoke, I started being afraid that I had emphysema.

The struggle continued. God continued to deal with me. Then, Satan was on the other side, pulling me in the other direction.

I never knew who the girl was, nor did I know any details, but one day in one of my classes, a certain girl became very sick in class. As they were helping her out of the room, one of the other girls said something to the effect, that she had some kind of heart trouble, and had a hole in her heart. To me, it sounded deftly like a nightmare and I felt terror inside of me that something like that would happen to me.

My rebellion against the school was still in effect. I did not do near as much damage as I did before.

Also, the war between Norman and I continued. So there I was, in a triangle of sorts. The war with the school. The war with Norman. Then the war that God and Satan were fighting over me.

I started doing a lot of telephone pranks. I would call the lumber company, or the glass company, or some other company, and place an order to be sent to Valley Point High School. I would always give phony names. A lot of the companies probably saw through it, and called the school to verify that it was a valid order. But one evening, when we were in one of our classrooms, I looked out the window and saw a load of lumber coming in. Shane and I went into the bathroom on the lower left wing, and spied out the window. The driver was talking to Mr. Vining. Mr. Vining was looking up at him as if he was wondering what he was doing there. Then we went back into the room where we were, and then in a few minutes, I saw the lumber leaving, the same way it came.

I remember once, early in the morning before school, that I was hanging around the lower left wing across from Mr. Vining's shop. Eric Phillips came up to me and said something about Mr. Vining, that I did not understand at the time.

He said to me, "If he likes you, he likes you. But if he don't, he don't."

But later on, I found out what he meant. I really liked Mr. Vining, and I passed the first year of agriculture. But in the second year, he turned against me, seemingly for no reason. I could tell that he didn't like me because of the way he would talk to me, that is, when he talked to me at all. I remember once, when he assigned us a job. We had to draw a line on a piece of wood and saw it off on the table saw, and leave a slither of line on the wood. Once, when I was fixing to cut a piece, he said to me sarcastically, "That's all right, you're not gonna hit it anyway."

A lot of times, he spoke to me in this sarcastic way. I remember once, that I was walking across the floor of the shop. Someone had carelessly left a fold-up ruler laying in the floor. I accidently tripped on it and broke it. He glared at me, saying, "I paid two dollars and eighty-five cents for that ruler."

During the first year, he let us do a project. We all built a nail box with sections in it. I did fairly well on that one. But in the second year, I could not learn anything from him. He did his best to discourage me all he could. That wasn't hard to do anyway. I guess because of the state of mind I already had toward school, it didn't take much to destroy any ambition that I may have had.

We continually tried to aggravate Mrs. Caldwell to some extent. I remember one time she said something to us to the effect, "I know you'all don't like to hear me gripe."

Then Jay Huges, that I knew in the fifth grade, sitting on the front row, spoke up and said, "Naw, I like for you to gripe at me."

I had this habit of belching in her class, just to aggravate her. One day after class, she called me over to the side and talked to me alone. She did not talk bad or hateful to me, she was polite, but all business like. She said to me, "Unless you have a note from a doctor saying you have a problem with belching, I don't wanna hear you do that in my class again." This is one of those things that is hard to explain, but when someone in authority, such as a teacher would talk to me in this manner, I respected them. So I didn't do it anymore.

But there was a new boy who was slim, and had brown hair, named Rodney that came to our class. He went too far at aggravating her. She corrected him one day for something and he talked back a little smart alecky, "Well, you don't have to be so blame gripy."

She told him that she would meet him in the office the next day. I remember after class, that Shane rebuked him for talking to her the way he did. He said to him something to the effect, "You shouldn't talk to her that way. We like to have fun with her, but you're going too far." I never said anything to Rodney myself, but I remember that I agreed with the things that Shane said.

In the tenth grade, I started working in the lunch room. My homeroom teacher's name was Mrs. Allison, a slim dark haired young lady probably in her thirties. The deal was, that we would get our meals free, and get paid two dollars a month. It wasn't much money, but we thought it was worth it, considering the fact that we ate free.

Now, during the time I worked in the lunch room, there was a certain boy who shared with me his recent experience with Jesus Christ; how he had gotton saved. He said to me, "It makes you feel real good."

I knew what he was talking about, because of my experience a few years earlier. But I had let Satan get such a grip on me I would not make a move in that direction.

We had to leave third period a little early to go to the lunch room to get started. My third period class was agriculture. We were usually in the shop, and I would always catch Mr. Vining's back turned, then go out the door to the lunch room. I always felt relieved when I got away from him.

Early one morning, a guy named Jack Mathis (Wayne's older brother) and I were fooling around at the south end of the main building. We were plotting to either throw a coke can or bottle into the building. I walked around behind the building to the lower left wing. Then, I threw a sprite bottle through the opened bathroom window. It busted all over the floor. As I was passing by the door, I heard the coke can clattering down the hall. He had opened the door at the south end and threw it down the hall. Right before this, it had been announced, that if anybody was caught doing any damage to the bathroom, in any way, they would be expelled.

That morning, during home room class, Mr. Monahan was making an announcement through the intercom. At the conclusion of the announcement, he said, "Send Robert Massingill to the office."

As I entered the office, I met Mr. Cline, and said, "I'm Robert Massingill."

Then, he called me out into the hall and asked me, "Do you have a way home?"

I answered, "No."

Then he asked me, "Do you know what you're called out here for?"

I answered, "No."

He looked at me suspiciously, and replied, "O Yes, you do." Then he went on to say, "Someone threw a coke bottle in this bathroom down here, and it busted all over the floor." As he was talking to me, he indicated with his finger, the bathroom on the lower left wing.

I denied it and said to the effect, "Well, it wasn't me. I was with Jack Mathis this morning."

He went back into the office for a minute, and left me standing in the hall. Then he came back out and asked me, "Which bathroom was it in, Robert?"

I replied, "Didn't you say it was in this bathroom down here?," referring to the one on the lower left wing.

He said, "No, I didn't say where it was."

I said, "Well, I donno."

He took me down to where it was. We walked into the bathroom and there laid the pieces of a sprite bottle scattered in the floor. I said, "It appears that somebody threw it through the window and it busted in the floor."

He said to me sharply, "It doesn't appear anything, big boy. You get smart with me and I'll have you sent home for good."

Sometime during the process of this, he went and talked to Jack. Jack confessed to throwing the coke can down the hall. Jack knew that I threw the bottle in the bathroom window, but he would not tell on me. He said to Mr. Cline, that he did not know anything about a coke bottle being thrown into the bathroom.

Mr. Cline said to me, "You've told me one lie. You said you were with Jack the whole time this morning. But you weren't with him all the time." Then he went on to say, "Jack admitted to what he did, he's cleaning up the broken glass." However, he said to me, "If you didn't do it, I don't blame you. I wouldn't take the blame for something I didn't do either. We're gonna let you go back to class now. But you're not gonna do anything else around here, we're gonna be watching you like a hawk."

There was a young boy named Claude Neighbors who lived in our neighborhood. He was slim and had lengthy black hair. He lived down the road from Zackary Wilmington. Zackary lived next door to Norman Price. At the back of our property, we had a strip of woods. Between our property line and Norman's house, there were two other residences.

It was now about the month of October of 1967. I never knew the exact details, but Claude and Stanley were doing some lawn mower trading. During the process of it, Stanley would send me to Claude's house to take him a lawn mower, or something of this sort. I was sort of caught in the middle, like a messenger. One sunny evening, I was at Stanley's house, and he had a lawn mower there. He said to me, "Robert, take this lawn mower down in the woods and hide it, and don't tell nobody where it's at."

I didn't ask him any questions. I took it down in the woods, waded into the middle of what I interpreted to be a large poison oak patch, and left it. (At this particular time, I did not break out with poison oak. It seems like after the ordeal with blood poison I had two years earlier, I had developed some sort of immunity against it. As far as I remember, I didn't break out with it for twenty-five years.) He didn't ask me where I hid it, and I didn't tell him.

The next day on the school bus, Stanley said to me, "Robert, when you get home this evening, stay inside the house. Don't answer the door for nobody."

I knew there was something fishy going on, and I figured it had something to do with the lawn mower that I had hidden in the woods. I did like Stanley said, at least for a little while. I peered out the window and saw Claude coming up the yard. He came up on the porch and knocked on the door. I hid in the bedroom and pretended I wasn't home.

But there was one small problem. I was out of chewing tobacco. In the middle of the subdivision, there was a small store. I traveled through the woods as far as I could. Then I had to take the road. In a few minutes, I met up with Norman Price, and with him was a whole bunch of other boys. As I was walking up the dirt road, next to a pine forest, he approached me and demanded to the effect, "Where's my lawn mower?"

I retorted using minor profanity, "I ain't got your lawn mower."

I had a bowie knife strapped on my belt. I never threathened him with it, but he must have thought I was going to. He said to me, "If you pull that knife on me, I'll take it away from you, and

I'll cut your throat with it!"

I got away from them (the boys with him were not threa-thening me, they were just following Norman), and ran through the woods. I climbed through a barbed wire fence, then stopped in a certain area, and caught my breath. After a few minutes, I traveled through the woods, following the same path I had previously followed. When I arrived across the road from our yard, I cleared a six foot bank, and landed in the road flat footed. Then, I crossed the road and went into the house. I went immediately to my bedroom closet and grabbed my 410 shotgun. I put a shell into the chamber, and then walked out on the porch. (About two years earlier, I had a .22 automatic rifle. While I was in the hospital with blood poison, Daddy traded it for the shotgun.) Then, I looked and there was Craig Wilmington coming up the yard. I asked him, "Where's Price?"

He replied, "I donno."

I said, "I'm gonna kill'im." Then, I went around the house, and down into the woods.

The first thoughts I had, were to go to his house and shoot him dead right there. I was planning to shoot him in the chest at close range. Within a few minutes, I was roaming in the woods, at the back of our property. As I was standing at the property line, I spied a man that looked like Norman behind the house next door. I started to shoot him, but then I saw that it wasn't Norman.

Then, Stanley and Zackary came walking through the woods. Apparently, they were looking for me. I told them that I was going to kill Norman as soon as I found him. Zackary told me that he wasn't home. He had gone to the school to pick up his brother. When Stanley saw that I was serious about killing him, he didn't want to hang around. He went home.

I said to Zackary, "When he gets home, go tell'im that I'm waiting on him with a stick." So Zackary agreed to do it.

About fifteen or twenty minutes later, Zackary returned. He said to me, "Robert, here he comes."

I was stooped down behind some boards that were the remains of a dog house, that I had built a year or so before. It had been torn down. I had found out that Norman was the one who did it.

I peered through a crack in the boards and saw his white T-shirt approaching. I let him get close enough for the shotgun to be effective. Then I raised up with the shotgun, and cocked the hammer back at the same time. He was carrying a large rounded broom handle about two feet long.

Everything began to happen so quickly. When he saw that I had a gun, he whirled around and shouted, "All right, Massingill!" Then, in an instant, I pulled the trigger. The gun fired, filling his right arm and the broom handle full of small birdshot. At the same time, Mike was on my left side and threw a spear at him. Then, I ran to the house.

When I was behind the house, among some cedar trees, Mike came running up and yelled something like, "You just made him mad! I saw blood running down his hand, and he's coming after you!" I reloaded the gun and waited. If he came up in the yard, I was planning to make sure the next shot hit him in the chest. But he never came. Then, Zackary came and told us that they had rushed him to the hospital.

A few minutes later, I went to the store and bought my chewing tobacco. At the time, Wayne Mathis was working at the store. As I was leaving the small store, with it's tin roof, I said to him, "I just shot Norman Price." As the rays from the late evening sun were making shadows over the landscape, he looked at me with a strange expression on his face and said nothing. (He told me later, that he didn't believe me.)

At the time this happened, Daddy was at work. I called and started explaining to him about what had just taken place. I asked him, "You know that Price boy?"

He said, "Yeah."

I said, "I shot'im while-ago."

He asked, "Well, did you kill'im?"

I said, "Naw, the shot hit his arm and they took him to the hospital."

Then, I heard him cuss on the other end of the phone. Then he said, "You stay in the house. I'll be down there after while, and see what's going on."

A little after dark, he pulled into the driveway in his black `60 Ford, and had a part time policeman with him. He got out of the car and was standing beside of it. I was standing in the yard. Then, he said to me in a deep, firm voice, "Get in!"

I answered, "Where are we going?"

"You're going to jail," he responded.

In a joking manner, I asked, "How long am I going to be there, ten years or twenty?"

Then, as far as I recall this scene, he replied to the effect, "Maybe ten."

They took me to jail and the Georgia Bureau of Investigation investigated the case.

The news spread all over the school about what had happened. The heading of a news column in the newspaper read, "Youth shot in dispute over mower."

There was a certain boy about my size named Howard that was in my ninth grade science class. (I was taking ninth grade science over again in the tenth grade.) One day in class, he raised his hand. Mr. Bailey asked him what he wanted. Then he asked, "Mr. Bailey, will they send you to reform school for shooting another boy?"

In sharp rebuke, Mr. Bailey said to him, "They'll send you to reform school for some of the things that you do. Like on the bus the other day, you were gonna beat the tar out of that boy (Mr. Bailey drove a bus and it so happened that Howard rode his bus).

Howard sheepishly grinned and replied, "I was gonna watch the other boy beat the tar out of him."

The case never came to trial. After about a year of haggling between my lawyer and the District Attorney's Office, they finally threw it out of court.

In January of 1968, I turned sixteen years old. That same month, I talked Mama into letting me quit school. I told her that I wanted to quit school. Then, she said to me, "You're gonna finish out this year anyway."

When she said that, I knew I was getting somewhere. I ended up quitting at the end of the week.   I stayed until pay-day. Then at lunch time, I got my two dollars and headed down the road through the woods, toward the railroad tracks.

CHAPTER EIGHT
THE FINAL PLAY

My rebellion toward the school did not end here. Although I did not have to go to school anymore, I still sought opportunities to get vengeance.

That following summer, I devised a plan to walk to the school, and try to set it on fire, or do any damage I could. As far as I remember, it was on a Friday night, I started walking to the school. I don't remember what all I was carrying on me, but I remember carrying a small jar of gasoline, and a machete. I barely was able to hide the machete under my shirt. The only thing covering the blade was the bottom of my shirt tail.

When I got to the railroad crossing at Five Springs Road, I began to feel uneasy about going, and I backed out. I headed back to where I was staying.

As I was walking up the road in the late night hours, a county patrol car with two deputies pulled up beside me. They asked me who I was, and where I was going.

I said, "I'm walking around the block."

"Walking around the block where?," they asked.

I don't remember what I said next, but I heard one of them say to the other, "We're not gonna get this straightened out, sitting here in the car."

Then, they both got out of the car and stood next to me. They asked me again where I was going. Then, I told them that I was going to stay all night at a friend's house. They asked me to the effect, "Have you seen any other suspicious people around here?"

I replied, "Yeah, I saw a car coming at me, and I thought it was gonna run over me." Actually I wasn't lying. I really did see the car. The car was half sliding in the gravel and seemed to have a flat tire.

Surprisingly enough, they believed me, and as if in a hurry, they took off toward the area, where I told them that I had seen the car.

I went the other way, and stayed off the road every time a car came by. Then I went on to where I was staying. Actually, I was not going to a friend's house. I slept on the wooden floor of a partly built house being constructed by a man that I worked for, part time.

Along about this time, Wayne Mathis and I got to be friends. Once on a summer night, he and I went loafing on foot. He had thick, lengthy brown hair. We walked all night, and I shared with him about the things I did in school. I said to him, "I took a medicine bottle full of gasoline to Mr. Todd's room, and set it on fire behind the radiator. I had a rifle bullet wrapped in it. But the glass didn't break."

He replied something to the effect, "You'd think it'd blow up, wouldn't you?"

I replied, "The next year, I used plastic." Then, I told him about the commode lid.

We devised a plot to go to the school and see how much damage we could do. A certain friend of ours had a car, and we all went riding one night. Our friend was under the influence of alcohol. We instructed him to drop us off in the dirt road behind the high school, and then, come back and pick us up in a few minutes. Then he drove away in his white compact Ford.

We went up behind the school, and I was carrying a slab of concrete that I found laying in the trail. Wayne carried some rocks. I slammed the concrete slab through the wired glass window in the door in the north left wing. At the same time, Wayne threw the rocks into the windows of the cafeteria. Then we ran back to the road and waited for our friend to pick us up. But he never did come back, so we had to walk home. This was the last strike I ever made against the school.

EPILOGUE

What causes us to do the things we do? What are the forces that we listen to as we run headlong toward destruction?

In the tenth chapter of the book of Daniel the prophet, Daniel tells us that demons rule kings and nations from the atmosphere. The demons do everything they can to hinder the work of God. They do everything they can to keep man from listening to God.

The Bible makes it clear to us that there is an age long war going on between good and evil; the war between God and Satan. The war is fought on a national, and on a world level. It is also fought on an individual level.

As the majority of the human race chooses the broad path that leads to destruction, the deadly game goes on. The drama will unfold itself before the universe until it's final climax.

There was once a story told about a certain criminal who was caught and sent to prison. He almost died in prison. One night Jesus appeared to him in a dream. In the dream, Jesus looked him in the eye with a penetrating gaze as if to draw poison out of a wound. After he awoke, his spiritual eyes were opened, and he accepted Jesus into his life.

Sometimes, we pray prayers that are wrong. I remember once, when I was about fourteen years old, I promised God that if He would let me live until I was grown, I would serve Him. Although I had good intentions, that prayer was wrong. I should have gotten saved then. The Bible says, "Now is the day of salvation" (11 Cor. 6:2). Although some prayers are wrong, sometimes God in His grace, answers them anyway.

In Genesis, Chapter Twenty-eight, Jacob prayed a prayer

that was somewhat illegal. He made God a promise that if he would prosper him in material things, he would serve Him. Even though the prayer was a little illegal, God answered it anyway.

God deals with man on man's level many times. In the twenty-first chapter of John's gospel, Jesus asked Peter, "Do you love Me?"

Peter answered, "Yes Lord, You know that I love You."

Jesus asked him this three times. But there is a catch to this. In the greek language, there are two different words for love. One is the higher level of love; the way God loves. The other is the lower level; the way man loves. When Jesus first asked Peter, "Do you love Me?" He was using the higher level of love. But when Peter answered, "Yes Lord, You know that I love You," he was using the lower level. The closest english equivalent would be, "Peter, do you love Me?" and Peter would answer, "Lord, You know that I like You." But what's interesting is the fact, that the third time Jesus asked him, "Do you love Me?, He used the lower level. He came down to Peter's level. In effect, He was saying, "Peter, do you like Me?"

God works on our level and answers our illegal prayers.

I remember once in the seventh grade, that Mrs. Boggs, a middle aged lady with dark hair, who was one of my spelling teachers, gave us an assignment to write our life story. I wrote of little simple things that I did around the house. I wrote that I did not go on vacation away from home, but I stayed home and played with the dogs we had for pets, and so forth.

Looking back, the story that I wrote was really a falsehood. Although the things that I wrote were true, my real life story was never told.

In March of 1972, after a long series of events, I finally gave my heart and life to The Lord. Then finally, the war had ended. The battle was over. The rebellious spirit was dead, and the demons had fled away. The Holy Spirit of The Living God came and dwelt in their place. The Light of The Son of God shined all around and dispelled the darkness.

Then as the prophecy said, "Bone came to his bone." The pieces supernaturally put themselves back together again.

Also, sometime afterwards I sent a letter to Norman Price and apologized to him for the things that had happened between us.

There was an Old Testament prophecy quoted in Matthew, Chapter Twelve, about Jesus. Verse Twenty says, "A bruised reed shall He not break, and smoking flax shall He not quench, till He send forth judgment unto victory."

The meaning is, that if Jesus sees the least spark of desire in a person to serve Him, He will not discourage it. It doesn't matter how many bad things a person has done, or how twisted things are in their life. It doesn't matter how much Satanic grip they are under, He will cause the spark to grow into a flame that will lead to eternal life.